Praise for **WHAT WENDELL WANTS**

"A winsome frolic... Lee has a winning way of confessing her absurdities, and, like many dog stories, tongue-in-cheek account reveals much about herself well as her wheaten terrier.... Obsessive or not, what there not to like about that?" —*Chicago Tribune*

"Indulgent pet owners will recognize themselves in Lee's funny tale of how her dog calls the shots."
—*Good Housekeeping* online

"*What Wendell Wants* will leave you laughing.... Dog people will recognize themselves in some of the ridiculous situations, such as planning holidays around the dog, discovering that the dog's haircut costs more than yours, and, if invited to a swanky affair, assuming the invitation includes the dog. Three paws up."
—*Cleveland Plain Dealer*

"Laugh-out-loud funny." —*Windsor Star*

"[Lee] may be crazy like a fox (terrier), but she writes like a pro. The odd, original, and totally unbelievable lengths she goes to are laugh-out-loud funny."
—*Dog Fancy*

"Hilarious... a perfect gift for the dog-crazy person in everyone's life." —*Edmonton Sun*

"You don't have to own a dog to apprec
the life of an openly obsessive dog own
laughing out loud in public places wh
book." —Nightsandweeken

"Nearly every dog owner will be able to relate to some part of Lee's comic exploration of her obsession with Wendell." —*Publishers Weekly*

Praise for **I DO. I DID. NOW WHAT?!**

"I loved Jenny's book. I related, I screamed, I smiled. It's terrifically funny, horribly true, and wonderfully tender at the same time."
—Laurie Notaro, best-selling author of
The Idiot Girls' Action-Adventure Club

"Were Candace Bushnell to chronicle her first year of marriage, it might look something like [this] frank, witty account of coming to terms with what matrimony really means." —*Publishers Weekly*

"Sharp observation and hilarious commentary . . . that should be passed out at pre-marriage counseling sessions as antidote to the poisonous advice of Dr. Laura."
—*Nashville City Paper*

"With candor and wit, Lee shares her experiences of marrying Mr. Right and finding out—well, what it's really like to have a husband." —*St. Petersburg Times*

"The perfect shower gift . . . self-help without the attitude . . . Plus, it's funny."
—*Milwaukee Journal Sentinel*

"A clever—and very funny—look at the psychic turmoil of petty annoyances of post-nuptial life."
—*Tucson Citizen*

Also by Jenny Lee

WHAT WENDELL WANTS
I DO. I DID. NOW WHAT?!

SKINNY

Bitching

A THIRTY-SOMETHING WOMAN MOUTHS OFF ABOUT
AGE ANGST, PREGNANCY PRESSURE, AND
THE DIETING BATTLES YOU'LL NEVER WIN

Jenny Lee

Delta Trade Paperbacks

SKINNY BITCHING
A Delta Trade Paperback / November 2005

Published by Bantam Dell
A Division of Random House, Inc.
New York, New York

Book design by Carol Malcolm Russo

Delta is a registered trademark of Random House, Inc.,
and the colophon is a trademark of Random House, Inc.

Library of Congress Cataloging in Publication Data
Lee, Jenny.
Skinny bitching : a thirty-something woman mouths off about baby guilt,
age angst, and the dieting battles you'll never win / Jenny Lee.
p. cm.
ISBN-13: 978-0-385-33787-8
ISBN-10: 0-385-33787-6
1. Women—Humor. 2. Aging—Humor.

PN6231.W6 L44 2005
814/.6 22   2005049385

Printed in the United States of America
Published simultaneously in Canada

www.bantamdell.com

BVG   10 9 8 7 6 5 4 3 2 1

In loving memory of my big sister,

Helen Yoon Lee (1965–1993).

Thanks for sharing your how-to-be-a-goddess wisdom with me

(love and laughter: do them both every damn day)

Contents

SKINNY

Bitching

Introduction

When I was in my twenties, of course, I longed to be in my thirties. I had read that all the angst I was feeling—*What the hell am I doing with my life? Do I have the right job? Do I have the right man? Do I have the right hair?*—would just melt away somehow as real life truly began. So when I finally hit thirty, I wasn't filled with dread and despair over my lost youth; on the contrary, I had a brazen bring-it-on attitude—bring on the respect of being thirty; bring on the perks of maturity; bring on the glam life, the successful career, the new marriage, the you-go-girl allure of a woman who, according to every magazine and HBO original programming, was just about to hit her sexual peak!

Yeah, right.

Obviously, I was too young then to know that I shouldn't have believed everything I read in the very same glossy rags whose headlines also happened to promise "Ten Days to Skinnier Thighs!" ...So there I was—a newly minted thirty-year-old (with the same fat thighs), and not only was I still subject to every damn bit of that old twenty-something angst, but now there was a whole new dimension to it:

I think I have the right job, but if I don't—it's too late to do anything about it! I damn well better have the right man, because we're married, so now I'm stuck with him.... The hell with having the RIGHT hair, what do I do about the seven GRAY hairs I just found?!!!

And, as if to add insult to injury, I found myself with a whole *new* slew of anxieties: some of them superficial beauty issues (*Should I start using eye cream? Where exactly does eye cream go? All around the eye, or just at the corner of the eye? And what if I get the eye cream IN my eye?*); some just about age (*I wonder if I'm too old to pull off this babydoll T-shirt? Maybe I'll just try it on. Are you kidding me, who can wear these stupid babydoll T-shirts; who are they sized for? Excuse me, miss—yeah, you with the exposed thong—do you work here? Well, do you have any larger sizes of this shirt? Because the medium I picked up wouldn't fit a Cabbage Patch doll. What's a Cabbage Patch doll? What do you MEAN what's a Cabbage Patch doll? When were you born? How old am I?? How old do you THINK I am? Wait, no—don't answer that. I'm thirtyish. NO, I didn't say thirty-SIX! I SAID THIRTY-ISH, MEANING I HAVE THE "ESSENCE" OF A*

WOMAN IN HER THIRTIES. WHAT DOES THAT MEAN? IT MEANS I'M OLD ENOUGH TO KNOW BETTER THAN TO WEAR A TINY LITTLE T-SHIRT THAT SAYS "ROCK STAR" ON IT. SO WHY DID I EVEN TRY THE DAMN THING ON???... You know, that's a very good question.); and there were even a few inklings of anxiety about headier things than shopping or catching up on the latest issue of *Us Weekly*—things like:

Am I satisfied with my accomplishments? What does it say about me that I actually believe that TiVo has changed my life? Am I still a feminist if I secretly bought a little T-shirt that says "Rock Star" on it and then proceeded to hide it in my bottom drawer? Will I be a good mother? Will I be one of those lame mothers who desperately tries to be her daughter's best friend only to have the whole thing backfire like it happened to Holly Hunter in the movie Thirteen? *Man, how great does Holly Hunter look now? She looks pretty hot for a woman in her forties—Michelle Pfeiffer, too... Hmmm, you know, I heard that your forties are pretty great...*

So basically what I've come to realize is that being a woman in the throes of her thirties is much more difficult than being a twenty-something, mainly because when you're in your twenties you have youth (and, perhaps more importantly, cluelessness) on your side. *So you still have to accept two hundred dollars a month from your mom for rent even though you are twenty-seven? Oh, that's okay; you're young; don't worry about it. Besides, everyone knows how expensive it is to live in the city.*

But when you're thirty-three and still living paycheck to

paycheck, and then you actually sit down to figure out your financial situation only to realize that, thanks to multiple credit cards and high interest rates, you're basically still paying off purchases you made in your twenties, your funny little motto of "Bills Suck" is no longer quite so amusing—particularly when it's *those* sucky little bills that are keeping you from buying an apartment or a house the way your more responsible thirty-something peers are doing. (Though it's hardly as if I have any open time slots in my general anxiety schedule *anyway* in order to stress over homeowner stuff like drapes, kitchen appliances, or trying to find all those decorative doodads that you always see in people's foyer bathrooms....)

Now by no means am I saying that everything about your thirties is bad. There are plenty—PLENTY—of things that are great about your thirties. Let's see: the fact that you now actually know what's on TV on a Friday night (oh, but perhaps that's one of those things you really shouldn't fess up to); that you no longer feel pressure to lie about the fact that you sometimes listen to Lite FM (apparently it's to be expected at this age); and perhaps the best thing about being a woman in your thirties is that when you walk around the beach and look at those skinny little teenage girls sucking down chili dogs, French fries, and ice cream like it's some kind of vacuum-cleaner convention, you get to savor the smug satisfaction of knowing they're going to pay for it later...*just like the rest of us*.

Just kidding (sorta). No, the best part about being a

thirty-something woman is the confidence you have gained by surviving all of those years of trying to figure out who you wanted to be (Madonna; whoever was sleeping with Brad Pitt; a princess in her twenties), so that, in the fullness of time, you could come into your own, to see who you really are (someone very articulate on the virtues of, say, the E-ZPass or TiVo ...).

The tricky part (and there's *always* a tricky part) is learning how to deal with all the flux that comes with your thirties—how you're pulled in ten different directions at once (who knew grown-ups had so many responsibilities?); how you never have time for yourself (I can finally afford pedicures now, but who's got the time?); and how you can no longer eat an entire bag of Doritos without having to pay for it later (though sometimes you just *have* to eat them).

This is where I'd use that analogy about cream rising to the top, except I can't really remember the quote (okay, full disclosure: You're a little flakier in the memory department, too, once you hit your third decade), but the gist of it is that you gotta make sure that you don't get lost in all the chaos of your thirties, because even though you're not young enough to pull off that micromini (were we *ever*, really?), it doesn't mean you aren't still young enough to go after everything you want to. So let's forget the whole cream analogy (it's really fattening, for one thing) and embrace a whole new attitude of "Old Enough to Know Better, But Ask Me if I Care" ...

But before you can get all sassy in your thirties, you first have to get to a point where you accept the fact that you've joined the ranks of adulthood by getting comfortable with the woman you've become.

Easier. Said. Than. Done.

Story. Of. My. Life.

Just like in those damn magazines that I'm so addicted to, everything is easier said than done. Want to look sexy? It's so *easy*; use more kohl around the eyes. Want to firm up those flabby thighs? Here are five *easy*-as-pie exercises you can do while sitting at your desk at work (never mind the two pieces of pie you ate for breakfast). Want to keep your man satisfied in bed? Here are fifteen *easy* things you can do if you've got the stamina of an Olympian and the flexibility of a ballerina.

Easy? Ha! Lies. Nothing is easy when you are a woman in your thirties, and the sooner we all accept this as gospel, the better off we'll all be. But don't think it's time to throw a big poor-me pity party, no, that's not necessary (those should be reserved for big pimples and bad-hair days), but you might want to buckle up because the road to reality is a little bumpy.

First, you must have a genuine meltdown, thirty-something style, which is the moment when you first realize that your twenties are gone and no cream (no matter how expensive or how much you use) is going to bring them back. Next, you have to give yourself a long hard look in the mirror (feel free to skip this stage, I did). Now it's time for the meat and potatoes (well, if you're doing the low-carb thing you can skip the potatoes), which means you now have to question all the different aspects of your life (physical and mental) and figure out what you're happy with, like the fact that you survived your twenties with your sanity intact and you finally have a hairstyle that you like. Next comes the hard part, which is dealing with all the issues that are still driving you batty, like the fact you're starting to lose hope that you'll ever lose those last ten pounds.

I have found the best way to deal with thirty-something angst is to challenge it head-on (think *Thelma & Louise*, well, without the driving-off-the-cliff part), by just getting it off your chest once and for all. Whining worked in our twenties, but now that you're in your thirties you've graduated to having full license to really bitch about the stuff that pisses you off. Rant and rave! Stomp your feet! Wave your arms! Do the hokey pokey if that's what you want to do. But just let it out, let it all out (this might take a while; hell, it took me twenty-seven chapters), and hopefully by the end you'll be able to laugh most of it off, because honestly, life is much too short to spend all our time worrying about how many calories were in the Krispy Kreme doughnut you just ate (there are certain things in life that you really shouldn't question); getting down on yourself for not going to the gym (you didn't go because working out sucks); or trying to understand your relationship with your mom (moms are supposed to drive you crazy, it's their job).

What I discovered (believe me, Einstein I'm not) is that it's easier to tackle all the superficial stuff first (yes, I get the irony of what I'm saying)—all the dumb stuff that is maxing out our angst schedule, things like what it means that we know what Nicole Kidman wore to the Oscars in 2000, but we couldn't name the twelfth president if we had a gun pointed at us. And my biggest beef (I'm doing the low-carb thing too) is why, oh WHY, do I spend so much time agonizing about my weight. Honestly, if I could just get back all those minutes spent obsessing about diets and exercise, I'd probably still be in my twenties! Well, word on the street is that there is more to life than being a size 4, so maybe if you unload all your baggage on the subject you'll feel much lighter.

Though once you get past all the surface stuff, you will now be faced with much headier issues—your career, your strained relationship with your mom, your husband, and oh yeah, that you're getting older by the second, and maybe it's time to start thinking about kids. But don't worry, this isn't like one of those magazine quizzes where you need to cheat to make sure you're labeled "sassy and cool"; no, as a woman in your thirties it's all mind over matter (and mind over gravity)—which means, if you're actually still hung up on wanting to be cool, then say the hell with what everyone else thinks and just know that you are cool (sorta).

Finally, once you've got everything figured out (trust me, it's soooo easy), you'll be ready for the final frontier (no, not the cliff), which is to celebrate the fact that you've earned the right to be a totally fabulous thirty-something woman who is a rock star (even without the babydoll T-shirt).

Prologue

I had a big joint birthday party with my friend Jenner to celebrate our thirtieth birthdays, never mind what year this was (you're never too young to start lying about your age). Anyway, my friend Phil (the only person I know who actually had a large enough apartment for a party of thirty people) was gracious enough to host what was supposed to be the party to end all parties, celebrating the new decade of our lives with our closest hundred-plus friends. But what happened, which oftentimes does when you have built up a particular event in your head (and charged six hundred dollars of booze on your credit card), was that real life got in the way—well, at least for me (Jenner, I'm pleased to report, had a stellar time at our joint birthday party). So instead of leading the bunny hop during Cyndi Lauper's "Girls Just Want to Have Fun," I was huddled in a corner with my husband stressing over the bad news we had received about his mother's health that day (I got the phone call when I was in a cab laughing about the fact that at the age of thirty I had just purchased my first keg).

But in a weird way, by missing out on my own thirtieth birthday party, I somehow just overlooked that I had reached my thirties. Well, not really, but my life at the time was just so busy that I sort of managed to conveniently forget....

Fast-forward a few years and I am in New York City with two female friends and we are out on a Saturday night past midnight (which, sadly, I hadn't done in a really long time). Earlier in the evening I had gone to a party on Park Avenue with a different friend and hung out with a bunch of couples in their early forties who talked an awful lot about their kids, expensive stereo systems, how HDTV changed their lives, and Led Zeppelin. I felt a little out of place—okay, fine, I'll admit it, I felt way younger than this crowd (please tell me that parties in your forties don't only consist of sitting around a very large flat-screen TV watching a Led Zeppelin concert on DVD)—and I was quite happy to leave at 11:00 P.M. and head back downtown to Nolita to continue my evening in a more juvenile manner.

So now it's close to one in the morning, and we're doing that thing where we are going from bar to bar trying to figure out which establishment should be so lucky as to host three lovely ladies who are hell-bent on having fun, but every place we go is either too crowded (I'm too old to stand at the bar; I like to sit down these days) or is filled with a bunch of twenty-something women wearing tight jeans and sexy little tops. Obviously, I was married, and I was with one woman who was engaged and another who was single but was so not in the mood to compete with visibly drunk girls who weren't even in high school when we were in college. Finally, after tromping around for a good twenty minutes past the point where I could pretend to be having fun, we ended up at Vig Bar, which was filled with a slightly older crowd (late twenties as opposed to the fake-ID college crowd), and we decided to settle in because they had a DJ that was playing good music (music that was popular in the eighties, thank you).

The place was dark, incredibly packed, and there were a lot of drunk guys who were singing at the top of their lungs and swaying (not to the music, but because they were sauced). After about ten minutes I was looking at my watch and thinking that I'd much rather be asleep than standing pressed up against the wall and hoping that someone wouldn't throw up on my shoes. I was out of cigarettes and had told the bouncer that I'd appreciate it if he flagged me when people went outside to smoke so I could mooch a cigarette off them. Thankfully, he was tall and was nice enough to give me the signal a few minutes later.

Outside it was snowing and cold and there were two girls who were lighting up. I politely asked if I could bum a smoke, and one of them said sure, if I'd let her wear my

Persian-lamb fur coat while outside. I thought it was a fair trade and agreed.

So we all stood there in silence for a while watching the snow, and finally I said, "Is it me, or are you guys really young? But then again, so is everyone in this place, huh?" I'm not sure why I said this, and in retrospect, it sounded slightly bitter and rude on my part (and maybe even a bit dumb, since one of them was wearing my very expensive coat), but I just couldn't help myself, since I was now in a mood that could only be described as out-of-sorts.

They both giggled a bit, and the one wearing funky hipster glasses and my coat (who you could just tell was a bit of a smart-ass—takes one to know one) spoke with more than a touch of bravado. "Please, we are both so old. We're practically almost twenty-five."

So it was my turn to giggle a bit, and say, "Twenty-five? My, that is old."

This of course invited them to ask me how old I was, and given the fact that I was now feeling like a total impostor in my own life (a woman caught between two decades), I said, "I'm thirty-three. Practically almost thirty-four."

I must say, I found myself surprised to hear my own age coming out of my mouth. But I was not as surprised as they were.

"THIRTY-THREE? YOU'RE THIRTY-THREE? DAMN, GIRLFRIEND, YOU LOOK GOOD FOR THIRTY-THREE. I CAN'T BELIEVE YOU'RE THIRTY-THREE. WOW. THAT'S SO OLD. MY

BROTHER IS THIRTY-FIVE AND HE'S MARRIED
AND HE LOOKS ANCIENT, LIKE AN OLD MAN.
AND YOU? WELL, YOU LOOK REALLY GREAT FOR
YOUR AGE. I CAN'T BELIEVE YOU'RE THIRTY-
THREE." This is the point when I'm already totally morti-
fied at having my age yelled out in the streets of New York,
but wait, it gets better (or worse, if you're a cynic). Because
then they start stopping people who are walking by and say-
ing things like, "HEY, CAN YOU BELIEVE THIS GIRL
IS THIRTY-THREE YEARS OLD? DOESN'T SHE
LOOK GREAT FOR HER AGE? SERIOUSLY, SHE'S
THIRTY-THREE YEARS OLD."

It was then that I finished my cigarette, retrieved my
coat, and walked back in the bar and promptly informed my
friends that I was leaving. Whoever said that getting older
meant getting wiser was right, because I knew that nothing
was going to salvage this night, and sometimes it's better to
quit while you're behind.

On the walk back to the apartment where I was staying, I
thought about the fact that I was indeed almost thirty-four,
which pretty much made me a thirty-something woman. It
was a little weird to think about my age, not as weird as having it bellowed out by two twenty-four-year-olds, but un-
nerving just the same.

I couldn't help but remember how smart and sophisticated I used to think I was when I was their exact age, living
in Manhattan, and being thrilled to be out late on a Saturday
night. It was then that I stopped in my tracks, and I noticed

that it had stopped snowing, and I realized that I was probably, finally, as smart and sophisticated as I once had believed myself to be back then. Yes, I was definitely no longer in my twenties, and even though it felt a little scary (God, would I have to start using eye cream now?), it wasn't too bad, mainly because I knew that I would soon get to go to bed.

SKINNY BITCHING:

Why I Hate Diets, Exercise, and

Anyone Skinnier than Me

At the age of thirty-three, I'm almost ready to give up on the fantasy of ever being a Skinny Bitch. How the whole Skinny Bitch thing works is like this: Any woman who's superskinny is a Skinny Bitch, and we hate her (all of us who are less skinny than she is). But just because we *hate* her doesn't mean that we wouldn't do just about anything to be skinny *like* her—and when I say "just about anything," I mean JUST ABOUT ANYTHING (well, besides actually eating a sensible diet and exercising every day, because, hey, we gotta draw the line somewhere)....

The most interesting thing to note about the whole Skinny Bitch concept is that it's completely relative. So what constitutes a Skinny Bitch to me is not necessarily what will do it for you. My husband once sweetly pointed out that if one were to be consistent about this approach, then I myself would be seen as a Skinny Bitch by those larger than me. After a moment's pause, I quickly waved off this idea. Because the whole Skinny Bitch philosophy is built on a way of thinking that is completely personal (and most certainly irrational). It's no comfort to *me* that I happen to be someone *else's* idea of a Skinny Bitch; I want to be my *own* idea of a Skinny Bitch. Which was where my husband threw his arms in the air, shook his head, and walked off, muttering under his breath, "Crazy bitch might be more apt."

"I HEARD THAT!" I yelled after him.

But I wasn't really mad. Because in a way he had a point.

I suck in my stomach whenever I get on my scale. Sure, I know it's irrational, but when it comes to women and their relationships with scales, there's no room for logic (I'm convinced that logic adds at least a pound or two). Once I'm on the scale, I immediately close my eyes. You'd think I could close my eyes first and *then* step on the scale, since it's right in front of me and only two inches off the ground, but once I misstepped and tipped the scale, managing to crash headfirst into my towel rack, which caused a bump that was definitely big enough to add some weight to my grand total, so I wasn't able to get on the scale for, like, a week, which in retrospect wasn't such a bad thing.

SO—once I'm safely on the scale, I take a deep breath, which I rapidly exhale in order to empty my lungs of all the air that my husband assures me doesn't weigh anything (listen, just because he was a physics major at MIT and is now a doctor doesn't necessarily mean he knows everything). It goes without saying that I'm totally buck-naked—no watch, no wedding ring, no hair bands—and, depending on the level of my pre-weigh-in dread, I may have even shaved my legs in preparation (no, my legs are not that hairy, but if a few epithelial cells can be all that stand in the way of getting caught for murder [I'm a big *CSI* fan], then they can certainly be the difference that'll tip the scale that one pound wherein lies the difference between utter wretchedness and your standard dissatisfaction). Cynical, I know, but you show me a woman who's an optimist when facing the scale, and I'll hold her skinny arms so we can both beat her senseless.

This is about when I open my eyes and stare at my bathroom wall a moment before my eyes make their journey downward and I begin singing a little song in my head that I wrote for just this occasion. It goes something like this: *please please please please please please please please please!!!* The nice thing about my lyrics is that they'll basically work with any tune.

Most days my weight is exactly what I'd expect it to be, and I have learned simply to accept it as a disappointing fact of life, since it's *always* been ten pounds over what I swear I'd be happy with; twenty pounds over what I'd sell my soul for; and thirty pounds over what I'd be if I were a celebrity with my own personal trainer, chef, and plastic surgeon. Now, granted, my weight has fluctuated by fifteen pounds throughout my twenties and early thirties, but my desire to lose ten for happiness and twenty for my soul has always remained more or less a constant.

Don't get me wrong—I'm certainly not complaining about the days when my weight is exactly what I expect it to be. Because those days when you get on the scale and are actually a pound or two *heavier* than what you thought you were are nothing short of a living hell (and, no, it's not water weight, because I don't even *get on* the scale the week before my period anymore, PMS and scales being a dangerous combination, not unlike PMS and chocolate).

The first thing I do on such days is give my scale a stern talking-to. "Oh, no you don't. Like *hell* I've gained two pounds." The second thing I do is get off the scale for a second or two and then get back on it (I'm nothing if not fair), and if it still reads the same, then I'm forced to take action.

Mainly this consists of moving my scale to a different part of the bathroom in hopes that the subtle shift in the slope of the floor may change the outcome in my favor—or perhaps my own placement in relation to, you know, the earth's gravitational pull (look, I know this makes no sense, but remember what I said about logic? Out the window and ready for a chalk outline on the sidewalk below, okay?). And don't smirk like that, because once in a while it works.

Next I decide that the scale may actually be extremely dirty, and may have accumulated some added dust weight or something. So out come the paper towels and Windex.

And then, if my last resort of trying to pee again fails, it's time to reach for the big guns....

It's a known fact that most new gym memberships are sold in the first two months of every year. Backed by New Year's resolutions and buoyed with hopeful determination, thousands of people march into their local gyms, year after year, only to peter out a month or two later, feeding the grim statistics. A chronic short-term gym-goer myself, I've spent the past ten years as such a statistic. But this year I decided I would *defy* the system:

Why should I even bother to join a gym on January 2, knowing full well that I'd stop going before spring was even officially declared? No, this year it was time to be strong. And I did hang tough for about two months—no gym!—before I finally caved in....

And now here I sit, grimly signing the bottom of the membership application while avoiding the glittering endorphin eyes of my "Membership Counselor," who is probably biting back her desire to chirp out something very perky about the fact that I still have *plenty* of time to get ready for "bikini season," which is just (giggle/snort) ten weeks away. But as she seems to be managing to keep herself in check, I give her a smile to show her that I'm a reasonably good sport. I know my place on the roulette wheel of urban gym membership, and I'm smart enough to know that the house always wins.

I'm always impressed by the strides in techno-evolution that health clubs make in the nine months or so that my membership lies fallow and then finally lapses. There are always more TVs than I remembered, bigger and flashier machines, and, of course, my favorite proof of the passage of time: an ever more bewildering number of new exercise classes that have sprung up since the previous year.

My first day at the gym is traditionally spent in the stretching area, lying on a mat with a towel sportily wrapped around my neck. It's here that I read through the monthly exercise-class schedule that is always Xeroxed on brightly colored paper (ooh—next month, how about yellow?!). Squinting to read the eight-point type, I mouth to myself these strange and wondrous titles—BalletCore, Urban Rebounding Express, Lo2Go—and then I flip to the other side of the page and read the class descriptions, marveling at the creative use of grammar and diction—all those sassy adjectives! those happy verbs! and those extra-perky exclamation marks!!! I stretch my neck muscles by craning to see whether I can properly ID the classes currently under way in the three different exercise studios on the floor.

Studio 1 at the back corner has twenty-plus women on individual mini-trampolines waving hand weights above their heads: Urban Rebounding Express (the trampolines are a dead giveaway). Studio 2 is trickier; the purple yoga mats make this look simple, but then you recall how, now that yoga is for the masses, there are just so many disciplines to choose from—Hatha, Vinyasa, or Kundalini. This class turns out to be Power Flex Yoga, the pupu platter of yoga classes, allowing one to sample all the types at once, with a fifteen-minute abs-only section, to boot.

Next I work my back muscles by sitting up to check out

Studio 3. But what I see makes me recoil and slam back down on my mat so fast that the woman on the lumbar ball next to me pauses, her arms only partly extended, her purple elasto-workout-band vaguely slack.

How could I have not remembered Studio 3? The one thing that never changes . . .

One of my problems with going to the gym—aside from the fact that I hate exercising, hate to sweat, hate how red my face gets while sweating, and hate always feeling like an impostor, even after blowing a month's salary at Niketown—is that I am truly scared of the "Women Who Spin."

Maybe "scared" isn't the right word, but it's something akin to that—some serious physiological reaction left over from the one time in my life when I really felt like I was going to die (this was before the shock paddles up front had become standard equipment)—and not in any graceful kind of a way, but in an *exercise room,* surrounded by a group of grunting, bike-seat–straddling women with thighs capable of splitting open an oil drum.

I still remember tasting the sweat pouring into my mouth from every single unclogged pore on my face, and my fervid prayers that the whole cliché of your life flashing before your eyes just before death would prove to be untrue—because otherwise my parting view of the world would be the inconceivably tight, fuchsia-thonged ass of the woman in front of me (my friend Jenner had advised me that the only way for a novice to make it through spinning was to position herself behind the best ass in the room—sort of an updated female version of the old horse-and-carrot trick).

Obviously, I didn't die that day, but I'm willing to put money down that it was only because my feet were so tightly strapped in, and because, since the front wheels of spinning bikes are weighted to ensure that you can't stop moving your legs, my poor heart continued to move strictly by the force of the rapid blood circulation.

But it was that class that showed me once and for all that I would never make "Featured Member of the Month" (especially since it was doubtful that a "featured member" would ever be the type to do conspiracy-theorist research on whether the government was putting together some type of elite secret undercover bionic militia of "Women Who Spin" for some random geopolitical reason).

As I open my eyes to dispel the image of that fateful day in my workout history, I lick my upper lip to taste a hint of salt commingling with my toner. I imagine the tiny beads of sweat standing at attention on my upper lip, a salute to the brave women of Studio 3 who at this very moment are "feeling the burn" in their glutes as they conquer some imaginary hill in the virtual countryside. I wonder if they know what I now know: how studies show weight training may be more beneficial than cardio; how, though men may find thongs sexy, the wedgied sight of them sometimes may also cause them to cringe involuntarily.

Lifting my face up off my now crinkled class schedule, I am pleased to note that there is a damp spot in the middle. Genuine sweat. Clear gold. And that means that my first workout of the year is officially over ("*Bee* wise! Slowly ease yourself into your new health regimen!" it says right on page 2 of "The *Buzz* on My New Gym" brochure. "Don't *Bee* unrealistic with your goals!!").

And how long will it be this time, I wonder, before I remember that the only way to beat the house at this place is to stay in the comfort of your very own home? Maybe not so very long. After all, with age comes experience.

Wow—could this be a new record for me in aborted gym attendance? Perhaps I'll even be featured on the "staff only" room's bulletin board: "Sucker Member of the Month." "She paid, but she didn't stay."

And, you know? Ask this stat if she cares!

GO DIRECTLY TO JAIL, MARTHA, DO NOT PASS GO, DO NOT COLLECT $200

I am not a good nester. I would be a lousy bird. Somehow I lack the ability to make a house a home. To be honest, I'm a little embarrassed by this fact and I was more than a little surprised at my inability to do so. I like to think that I have a keen eye for fashion, and some may even say that I have great personal style, but somehow I can't seem to project it onto my current surroundings.

I became aware of my problem in my twenties, after I got my first solo New York apartment. I of course blamed the apartment itself, first because it was long and narrow and shaped like a wine bottle, and second because the doorway was so small it couldn't fit my plush rose-colored couch that I had inherited from my mom after she moved to a smaller house. My theory at the time was that if your apartment couldn't even fit a couch in it, then how could it possibly ever become a real home? I suppose I could have just bought a smaller and more narrow couch, but I was stubborn and refused to give up my strict guidelines of what makes a good couch (I must be able to completely stretch out on it, and it must be cushiony enough to be a place where one could camp out for days at a time, if needed, with room to spare for plenty of books and magazines, a dog, and maybe even another person).

So for five years I remained couchless, and I thought of my apartment as more like a very large walk-in closet— simply a place to house all my clothes. I didn't even unpack all my boxes until my third year, and that was only because my best friend, Laura, took pity on me (or maybe the apartment) and helped me try to put it in some semblance of order. But even after we finished, it still seemed lacking.

I now know that it was me, and not the apartment, because a friend took over my lease when I left New York and I visited her a few years ago and was totally blown away by what she had done with the place. She had transformed my extra-large walk-in closet with bathroom into a real cozy enclave, a love nest actually for her and her girlfriend.

My second revelation that I was an incompetent nester (stubborn people need at least two examples, because the first instance can always be written off as a fluke) came when I started a book club in my current apartment building. I put up signs in the middle of winter to see if anyone had any interest in joining a lazy person's dream book club (where you wouldn't have to leave the building and everyone solemnly swore that no one would get dissed if they didn't read the book), and ended up with a ten-person group. We took turns selecting the books to read as well as hosting, so I got to see a lot of my neighbors' apartments. I live in a four-story walk-up and each floor contains two two-bedroom apartments, two one-bedroom (with small study) apartments, and one studio, all with identical layouts from floor to floor. And what I discovered was that everyone in the book club had these cozy, well-decorated apartments—well, everyone except for me. Nor could I use disposable income as an excuse; after all, the two women who shared an apartment on the floor below me were only two years out of college and lived on a far smaller budget than I did, and their apartment was great.

I only wish I could say that some of their design inspiration actually rubbed off on me. I mean, I was president of the book club, and I dreaded having everyone over to see our place. (After they left, the nicest thing they could say was that I made the most out of my tiny kitchen because I sure knew how to bake; when in doubt, overcompensate with good food, I always say.) I mean sure we have all the basic furniture that one needs, and God knows we have plenty of other stuff (I'm a big shopper). But somehow it just lacks that pulled-together look of being a grown-up apartment (and it lacks charm). So where my neighbors' apartments spoke volumes about their lives (she's keeping Pottery Barn in business, he's Mr. Joe Bachelor), I'm not certain our apartment said all that much about us as a couple—well, beyond the fact that we probably don't seem as messy as we are. Our apartment is a very odd mixture of random stuff that is perfectly nice on its own but doesn't quite work when all put together.

I am more than willing to take the majority of the blame for this problem, because before we were married my husband had his own apartment in New York, which was wonderfully decorated (though his mother might have been the one to thank) and well suited to his image of Young Bachelor in Medical School with Very Generous Parents. I can't even pass the buck to my genes, because my mother has fabulous home-decorating skills too; my childhood bedroom always matched perfectly, down to the dust ruffle and the little tassel thingie that hung from the curtains.

So obviously the problem lies with me. And because I do happen to be married, the problem now had another tenant as well.

"What do you think it says about me as a person that our apartment isn't all that great looking?"

This question probably ranks very high on my husband's list of dangerous places that should never be visited (akin to being in the bathroom with me when I get on the scale, or taking a dare to walk across a "frozen" lake). Given this, my husband refuses to even acknowledge that I have said anything at all.

"Cosmas, did you hear me?" I ask. I just can't help myself.

He shakes his head no. No, he's going to lie and pretend that he didn't hear me. No, he really doesn't want to answer the question he hasn't heard. No, he realizes that he has no way out because I happen to be closer to the door.

"Nothing is wrong with our apartment. We're just messy." Nice move using the plural first person.

"Do you think I have a problem with permanence?"

My new line of questioning has gone from dangerous (ten minutes to placate me) to deadly (half hour and counting to placate), and though Cosmas is a doctor and has dealt with a few life-and-death situations in his day, he's never one to take the death of his precious free time too lightly. It is time to defuse the situation, and he speaks with bomb-squad precision.

"I think our current living situation, which I must repeat is totally fine by me," he says, squeezing his eyes shut reflexively, "probably has more to do with a lack of effort versus lack of commitment."

I think about what he just said, and it makes a lot of sense (though I'm not sure I want to immediately admit this). And if I were to extrapolate a point out of his seemingly wise but cryptic statement (which is of course his intention), I could concede that we never made our current living space a high priority in our lives, and had given the majority of our time to our respective careers and to seeing a lot of movies.

I push forward with my questioning. "So what do you think it says about our relationship that we don't make the effort to have a nice home together?"

Cosmas stands up at this point, gives me a shake of the head, and excuses himself to the bathroom, the one room in our apartment that is more than comfortable due to our multitude of magazine subscriptions and a really great bath-room rug. Honestly, you could spend a day in there and be fine. He is hoping that he can figuratively, as well as literally, shut the door on this conversation altogether.

I don't pursue him. Mainly because I know that this is something I am going to have to figure out for myself. It's my own personal head trip of the moment and it's up to me to find my way home. I begin to contemplate whether I should go to the local library and do a little research on the nesting habits of birds, thinking that maybe I can find some parallels. But I think better of this, because I know I will more than likely just read that it's mainly the female birds who are in charge of the nest building (why should it be any different in any other species?), and that it is instinctual for the birds because they need a place to lay their eggs. And as much as I think that there is a lot to be said about human evolution and the profoundness of the animal kingdom, yada-yada (I've learned a lot from my dog, Wendell), I'm not sure if I can really learn that much from our feathered friends when it comes to me and my own nesting instincts, or rather, the lack thereof.

I decide instead to go straight to the source—literally bow before the queen herself to see what she might have to say—and pick up the latest issue of *Martha Stewart Living* at the newsstand in Harvard Square. Believe me when I say that I am a certifiable magazine junkie, but this is the one magazine I avoid at all costs. (Aha, maybe it is psychologi-cal. Fear of Martha Stewart causes woman to lose nesting instincts!) I remember flipping through one in a doctor's-office waiting room, and to this very day I can visualize the exact article that freaked me out. It was a feature on how to redecorate your laundry room, and though I didn't have one at the time, I foolishly thought that it might be interesting to learn about for the future. Anyway, she had suggested buying large glass jars with lids (like I even know where one buys such jars) for your laundry detergent, allowing you to get rid of the ugly cardboard boxes that laundry detergent is sold in that you never knew offended you. She also advised pitching the plastic scoopers too, favoring cute mugs or sleek stainless-steel scoops. Wait, there's more. As the great finale for this particular project (don't even get me started on the three-tiered dirty-clothes-basket system), she wanted you to dig out your stencil kit (I keep mine in my hall closet, where do you keep yours?) so you could decorate and correctly label each canister (obviously so your housekeeper wouldn't ruin your wash). By the end of the article, I'm sure I looked even more ill than when I first arrived.

I remembered feeling so completely inadequate right at that very moment, because never in a million years—and I do consider myself to be quite creative and spiritedly resourceful—would I have ever thought about redecorating my laundry room (if I had one), and I'm not just saying that I wouldn't choose to redecorate it in the way that she suggested, but that I wouldn't choose to decorate it the first time around. And honestly, what woman has the extra fifty hours on her hands—what with working, taking care of her kids, dealing with her husband, buying birthday cards, and keeping up on trite celebrity gossip—to actually give to such a project? Show me the woman who's got the time, and I'll show you a woman who's on meth.

I'm sitting on a bench in Cambridge Common Park near my house, and I have a brown paper bag in my lap that, at first glance, might appear to contain porn (probably because I'm holding it with sweaty palms). Having just relived that memory, I am suddenly reluctant to open the magazine at all. In fact, maybe my whole block against home decorating in general came from that one previous traumatic experience. Maybe that one article totally overstimulated the part of my brain that is responsible for home décor, and a "fuse" was blown. Yes, perhaps I should stop blaming myself and instead blame Martha, who happens to as of this writing be behind bars (though some speculate that she's just being used as a backlash against big-business greed, I can't help but wonder whether a bunch of powerful women who were sick of being made to feel inadequate in the wake of her domestic glory might have pulled a few strings of their own just so they could get a breather for a change).

I mean, after all, I do remember telling quite a few friends about my one bad magazine experience and declaring that the day I started caring about laundry-detergent presentation would be a great day to go ice-skating in hell.

I look down at the brown paper bag still in my lap. Was this it? Were the penguins of purgatory rubbing their little flippers together in anticipation of a nice freeze that would allow them to bobsled down to hell? Maybe I could blame my bravado on the fact that I probably spent too much time in my twenties in Manhattan bars (remember, I didn't have a couch), and in a dark, smoky bar it's pretty hard to see ahead to the future when you would ever be on the other side of the window walking by and wondering how those young people managed to spend so much time in bars as opposed to in their own homes on their own mismatched living-room couches. Perhaps I was too tough on Martha, as I know quite a few women who really respect her creativity and advice (though I guarantee she still makes them feel somewhat inadequate), and maybe I was just being petty to put all the blame on her. Maybe the reason why my house wasn't "done" was because I spent too much time on park benches contemplating my life as opposed to living it, or rather decorating it. You think?

I get up and decide to go home, and as I pass a garbage can I do think about tossing in the magazine, but I don't. I'm not sure if I'm going to read it—obviously, I still had issues—but at least I could put it in the bathroom, strictly as decoration.

CHAMPAGNE TASTE

I don't even like champagne. I find it sour—so much so that I make a face when I drink it (and not a cute face; more like the face of a woman who's about to choke on a little bubble of CO_2). Maybe I just haven't tried the good stuff. I guess I'm talking Cristal here. But it's funny, because my mom's favorite thing to say to me after I moved to New York and began to get sucked into the glamour of it all was, "You have champagne taste." And this wasn't a compliment. She really believed that what she saw as my expensive taste was going to hinder me from ever finding a husband.

"Men don't like women who *have champagne taste*," she would say.

At first I thought she was just saying this so she wouldn't

have to buy me the latest handbag that I was coveting, but after a while I realized this was something she believed to her very core.

Of course, I tried to respond in a logical fashion—"Mom, I don't even like champagne." But logic, I guess, had nothing to do with it.

"It's bad to want too much," she'd tell me.

Surely what my mom needed was to sit in on one of the women's-studies classes I had taken in college. Now, there was a group of women who wanted too much. And these women didn't just want things for themselves; they wanted things for *all* women. This was admirable, of course, but totally unrealistic, in my view. Sure, I thought men and women should enjoy equal rights, but the problem lay in the fact that men and women are very different, so it's sort of hard to figure out big-picture equality at times.

I should mention that I was taking these classes in the early '90s, when women were finally getting somewhere, and the mantra was that you could have it all. You could have the great career. You could have a husband and kids, too. You could have an SUV for the week and a convertible roadster for the weekends.

This I liked. I was very big into having it all at the time. It just made sense that a person should be able to have anything she wants—well, as long as she doesn't expect it to be *handed* to her. Sure, I had a big appetite for life, and yes, I was totally materialistic, but I never expected that my desires were something that needed to be fulfilled by another—and certainly not a man.

It was this thought that made me bristle every time the topic came up with my mom. She was of a generation (and culture) that had learned to accept that men were dominant and women were subservient. Now, my mom was no shrinking violet, mind you. No, she knew how to get what she wanted—big houses, nice furniture, children who made straight A's. But she paid a price for it. My dad was a surgeon and made the big bucks, while my mom stayed at home and spent them. And there's no question my dad benefited, since the man never had to cook a meal, wash clothes, or do anything else even remotely domestic around the house. I suppose both of them got what they wanted. Except that my mom also got a daughter who was completely antiestablishment when it came to this male-female dynamic.

My mom had married at the age of twenty-six, which was statistically late for women in Korea forty years ago. She said that she had been saved from being an old maid when my dad asked for her hand in marriage and felt truly fortunate. I remember trembling a little when she told me this—trembling, that is, so as not to roll my eyes like I wanted to and shout, "Are you kidding me? That's the dumbest thing I ever heard!" But I was not raised to be disrespectful, so I kept my mouth shut. (Besides, I was really close to convincing her to buy me a Prada purse, so who was I to rock the boat?)

So by the time I turned twenty-six and was still unmarried, my mother was spending a lot of time worrying about my future. She clucked her tongue all the time and said that she just wouldn't be able to relax until her daughter had a man to take care of her. Seriously, that's what she said. And my response was always, "I don't need a man to take care of me." We'd go round and round like a broken record.

"You need to get married and have a man take care of you."

"No, I don't. I don't *need* a man to take care of me."

"Tsk. Tsk. I wonder what man is going to want to marry a woman with such *champagne taste*."

"Mom, I'm not really interested in getting married to a man who would *care*."

"If only you had a man to take care of you, I wouldn't worry."

"Don't worry about me, I don't need a *man* to take care of me."

"You should change your lipstick too, it's *too dark*. Men like women in pink lipstick. How do you expect to find a man to take care of you wearing such *dark* lipstick?"

"Any man that cares more about my lipstick than my brain can go jump off a bridge. I don't need a man to take *care* of me. I'm doing fine on my own, thank you."

"If you got married, maybe your husband would buy you a Prada purse."

"I don't need a *man* to buy me a Prada purse. I have *you* to buy it for me."

And inevitably we'd end up right back where we started, which was nowhere. We were at an impasse between two different generations, two different cultures, and two different Prada purses (I really wanted the more expensive one, but my mom felt that it was too showy, and would scare off potential suitors).

After a while we learned not to talk about it, because no matter how we tried, we could never get the other person to understand. I knew that my mom loved me and only wanted what was best for me, and that she simply felt (strongly) that having a husband would keep me safe and secure. But I just didn't see it that way. I wanted to have it all on my own, on my own terms, and I didn't care if I had to work my ass off to get it. I DID NOT NEED A MAN TO TAKE CARE OF ME.

Stubborn. Like mules, we were.

In the late '90s, the tide of feminism-lite (which is what I'd come to call it) had started to shift, and the natives were growing restless. Women everywhere were starting to get a little fed up with trying to have it all, mainly because they were completely stressed and exhausted. Trying to juggle a career and a family was proving to be difficult, not for lack of will, or even ability, but more because they were getting their capes mixed up. Were they Super Career Woman? Were they Super Mom? Were they Super Wife? Or were they just super insane?

Perhaps this will always be a struggle for us. . . . And, man, did I struggle after I finally got married. Hell, I'm still struggling. Some days I wake up and I still want it all, and I still believe I can have it. And other days I wake up and I feel like I'd be lucky if I could even get halfway down my to-do list. Some days I wake up and am happy to take care of my husband. Other days I wake up and want to shoot him. Some days I wake up and decide that maybe my mother was right, after all, and maybe I *do* just want a man to take care of me (or at least take out the trash regularly and clean the car every now and again). And then some days I just wake up feeling tired.

Ah, but then, once every so often, there are the days again, when I wake up and think that most anything is possible—like starting a revolution, getting through my entire to-do list, or maybe finding champagne that I actually *like*. Fine, so my mom likes to say I have champagne taste. And while this used to really bug the crap out of me (especially when used as an excuse not to buy me something), now I see it as a compliment. Hey, I'm a fabulous woman who just so happens to have good taste. And sure it's great when I get nice things as gifts, but I'm certainly not averse to working hard and getting the money to buy things for myself, too. I mean, why *can't* a woman have it all?

THE CHICKEN-FRIED TRUTH

I wish I were one of those people who sleeps naked. Not because I'm a big exhibitionist or anything, but I feel like if you can sleep naked, then you must be very comfortable with your body (or at least you must have a really good lock on your bedroom door). Of course, there was a time in my twenties when maybe I slept naked a few nights here or there—and it was not that I was too busy being a slut to remember where my clothes actually were; not at all. I was probably just in one of those oh-so-fleeting periods when I was actually feeling skinny (because God knows if you have company, that's all the more reason not to parade about naked, right?).

Anyway, it's been a long time since I did the whole

naked-as-a-jaybird thing. These days I no longer even want to walk to the *bathroom* naked. I mean, it's just my husband, my dog, and me, so ostensibly if I happened to wake up in the middle of the night and had to go pee, I could do so without fear of running into someone who shouldn't see me. But, again, I don't want to.

You know, it's one thing to not be brave enough to stare at yourself in a mirror naked in the light of day, but it's a whole other issue if you won't walk in the dark to the bathroom in the middle of the night when no one is even going to see you (and I assure you, both my husband and our dog are heavy sleepers).

It just so happens that I'm in bed in the middle of the night, when all this occurs to me. And I'm sure this is a direct result of the fact that I currently need to go to the bathroom (though it is the middle of winter, and let me tell you, it's freakin' cold in Massachusetts in the winter—so, the apartment is cold, the floor is cold, and you can damn well be sure that the toilet is going to be *arctic* cold). I just do not feel like leaving my warm bed. And then, right as I'm about to flip the duvet back (if you have to go, you have to go), I realize I'm naked.

When you first realize that you're naked without remembering why, you always feel a little weirded out. I mean, it's dark, you're disoriented, you realize you're naked, *and* there is also someone in the bed with you. So you have that tiny fraction of a second where you wonder if you happen to be a famous rock star who partied too hard the night before and maybe now you don't remember which famous male model you took home and got naked with, but then your eyes begin to focus, and you recognize the familiar lump that makes up your husband. This is when you let out the breath you were holding in and you think, *That's right, I'm not a famous rock star, and that's not a male model* (sometimes you are happy about this, and sometimes you aren't). Anyway, now that you've established *who* you are, *where* you are, and the fact that you are indeed naked, it's time to try to figure out why.

Well, you certainly have an inkling. Rewind to a month ago, when you were standing in the Bloomingdale's home-furnishings department with your husband, picking out a new down comforter. The down comforter that you've been sleeping under since college has become—what's the word? Oh, that's right, disgusting—so you have trashed it, deciding that it's finally time to get a new one. What you didn't know is how ridiculously expensive down comforters have now become, and you're sort of staring at the price tags of the different ones on display and calculating all the other things you could buy for yourself with the same amount of money. After a while you pick out a very lightweight comforter, which is very expensive, even though it clearly has far less down in it than the other ones (maybe there's some kind of hierarchy in the duck world, too?), and you are about to purchase it when your husband comes walking up with a different comforter in his arms. Now, I know that most husbands don't like to shop, especially in the home-furnishings department, but my husband is not like most husbands. No, Cosmas is actually really *into* home-furnishings stuff. He likes expensive sheets; he likes big, fluffy towels; and he can really appreciate a good sale.

So there you are, both of you face-to-face, armed with competing down comforters. It's like a shoot-out in the Wild West, only not.

He eyes mine. "Yours looks a little thin."

I roll my eyes back. "The good ones *are* thin; if they're too thick, they'll be too hot and you'll sweat a lot and..."

He's heard enough, and holds his hand up to stop me. Not liking to talk about sweating (he thinks it's gross), he nods. Round 1 to Jenny.

I get to go first. "Mine's summer-weight, but we can use it all year round."

He looks at his tag. "Well, mine is actually labeled a 'year-round' weight, which means that it was really made to be used all year round."

Rather than getting into a long drawn-out explanation of the fact that using a summer-weight all year round is also standard practice (and even advised by some experts. I know this, as I read it somewhere), I decide it isn't worth it. I take a different tack.

"Are you sure yours is year-round? It looks pretty heavy, and you know I hate to be hot when I sleep."

He thrusts a tag in my face, and I can see that, yes, the one he is holding is, indeed, labeled a "year-round" weight. Still, I have my doubts.

I go for the cheap shot. "Did you remember to get a queen size?" Looking at sizes is something that I could easily see him forgetting to do.

He gives me a smug nod and then needles back. "Did *you*?"

"Of course I did." I find myself rapidly tiring of this exchange. "Fine, how much is yours?"

"On sale for ninety-nine ninety-nine."

Wow, his is cheap, too.

He taps his foot impatiently.

"Um, mine's six fifty," I mumble, hoping the price will sound less expensive, but he's leaned in and hears me perfectly.

"Six hundred and fifty dollars? Are you high?"

So then I launch into the fact that mine is one of the top brands, and that it's famous for its thousand-year warranty (okay, I'm grasping here, but whatever), and a good comforter is just not something you scrimp on, because sleep is *so* important, blah blah blah. By the end of my discourse, I've dropped mine on the floor and grabbed for his, suspicious that it might be mismarked, or maybe his isn't even real duck down—maybe it's the down from some cheap trailer-park turkeys, or is some kind of, you know, "down" that has been creatively spelled "doun," since it's manufactured in Bhopal.

Turns out his comforter has simply been discontinued, hence the low, low price. Having read the label, I have to admit it seems like a pretty good deal, but it still looks a little thick to me. I worry that it might be too hot for us, and that I'll just be forced to drive back out to exchange it for another one, which I know I'll never do, because I'd probably lose the receipt and keep putting it off until it's too late.

I decide to cover my bases. "Yours looks good, but it's sorta thickish. What if it makes us too hot? You know I hate to be hot when I sleep." I keep repeating this, trying to indicate as gently as possible that my being too hot is going to be his problem, too, because when I get too hot, I wake up more often in the middle of the night, and when I wake up in the middle of the night I always have to pee, and when I have to get up to go pee I may not be able to go back to sleep, and if I can't go back to sleep ... well, then I'll have to wake him up because I'll be bored.

Cosmas does a quick calculation in his head and decides that saving five hundred dollars is probably worth a little missed sleep on his part. Besides, he probably thinks I'm just being my normal melodramatic self.

Clearly not.

So what's happened on this disorientingly naked night is that I got so hot from sleeping under this big fat *liar* of a comforter (year-round, my ass—I mean, sure, if you happen to live in Antarctica) that I must have stripped down while asleep, and now, here I am, too warm, wide-awake, needing to pee, and—that's right, buck-naked. I consider waking Cosmas up just for spite; obviously, it's his fault that I'm in this predicament to begin with, because if he hadn't won the comforter shoot-out, I wouldn't be lying here naked, analyzing why I'm reluctant to walk ten feet in the buff.

I guess the main reason I'm feeling shy about walking naked to my own bathroom is that I'm feeling a little, oh, how should I put this delicately, uh, *fat*. There, I said it. I'm feeling fat and now I'm not even comfortable in my own body, which is a really sad place to be. I mean, as much as I buy into the whole skinny-version of fabulous America by reading every entertainment magazine known to man, I do find the current obsession with weight a bit sad, not to mention ironic, as the majority of people outside of L.A. and NYC are, in fact, only getting more obese by the year.

Let the record state that I am *not* obese. But, like most women, I could stand to lose five or ten (oh, let's round up and say—*twenty*) pounds. But I don't think it's so much the numbers on the scale that are the problem; it's more my own notion of what I think about myself. I mean, so what if I'm a little full in the face (truth be told, I'd only be fat if I were a celebrity, and if I still lived in New York I'd be, I guess, "plump," which probably means that by any normal standard, I'm not far from average). No amount of weight should be enough to topple someone's self-esteem. Especially in the dark!

I remember reading some women's magazine that recommended a little exercise in which you were supposed to find something positive to say about every part of your body, rather than pointing out the flaws, and that in doing so you would have a better self-image. I decide to do a lightning round of it in my head.

Ready. Set. Go:

I like the fact that after a pedicure I have pretty good-looking feet (my toes are well-proportioned and I have great taste in nail polish). Um...in a similar vein, my hands are fine, too. Ah...okay, this isn't working, because if all

I've got to be proud of are my hands and my feet, then I'm going to start making showering in the dark a full-time arrangement. Then I decide that I have an okay back (it's not all hunched over, anyway, and my waist still plunges in a *little*). I move around to my front and decide that although my stomach may not be as flat as it once was, it's still *"flat-ish"* if in a slightly rounded sort of way. And as far as my bustline, well, I never had much of one to begin with, and that certainly hasn't changed, so there's not much to think about there (take that, gravity; I've got nothing for you to grab hold of!). Now it's time to go low. My butt—oh, my butt... well, it's not flat, that's for sure, but it's not wide like a Mack truck either. It may even be a bit big, but then, thank God for J.Lo and Beyoncé, who have somehow managed to bring big butts back in!

And then, finally, it's thigh time. I wonder if I can get away with the Thumper-rabbit clause when it comes to this issue (you know, if you can't say anything nice about some-one, then you shouldn't say anything at all). Probably not. Okay, I *really* have to pee now. So I put on my positive-thinking cap and decide that if I happened to be a chicken who was growing up to be a piece of fried chicken in a fast-food joint, my large thighs would probably be seen as a wel-come attribute.

Poof. It's like a magical spell has broken—suddenly I feel pretty good about my body (or maybe it's just the thought of fried chicken that is making me happy), and I think to myself, *The hell with being ashamed of it. I'm going to walk to the bathroom to pee, and, dammit, I'm going to do it with pride.*

I dig myself out from under the comforter from hell, consider turning on the light (before deciding wisely that I probably ought to take baby steps here), and off I go, chicken-fried thighs and all.

THAT SINKING FEELING

After four years of marriage, it's probably pretty natural that things start to slow down a bit, so when Cosmas said he was in the mood, I knew that I had to move fast. There was a time when I was always in the mood, but after getting rejected often enough I stopped asking. Eventually, you learn to live without it, which sounds depressing, but it isn't so bad. It's almost as if you forget about the adrenaline highs that are involved, and if you want to know the truth, it's been a long time for us.

So before he can change his mind, I'm scrambling off the couch and racing toward the bedroom; I call out over my shoulder, "Ooooh, wanna play by candlelight?"

"Won't that be too dark?" He reconsiders for a second,

noting my excitement, and probably feeling guilty that it's been so long. "Okay, why not, there's always a first for everything."

So after about ten minutes of searching for candles, matches, and getting the game all set up, we're ready to go.

I always like to go first and Cosmas usually lets me, but before I can call out my first missile strike, he stops me.

"If you win, you have to show your board at the end of the game. Okay?"

Ah, now I remember why we haven't played Battleship in so long (we play the original one, not the electronic version, as I prefer to make my own explosion noises); because the last time we played best two out of three and I won two straight games, we got into a fight over the fact that Cosmas wanted me to show him where I had placed my little two-person sub, which he wasn't able to locate in Game 1 or in Game 2, and I refused. He then accused me of bad sportsmanship and I accused him of being a sore loser. He called me a baby, and I called him a big meanie, and then I "accidentally" snapped the lid closed on his finger (I'm going to claim self-defense, because he tried to grab my control panel to peek, and I'm positive that any naval commander would have done the same).

His point was that we were just playing a game, and so my being secretive about it took my competitiveness from a little annoying to the height of totally off-putting. While I understood his view on the matter, I also found it completely illogical. Battleship is a game of strategic placement of your own ships as well as strategic guesses as to where your opponent has placed his, and obviously my secret strategy with my two-person sub was working in my favor (it won me both games), and by me having to show him where I placed it (the same place, both times), I would be basically sinking my own advantage. But when I tried to explain my side, he wouldn't even listen. I tried to flip the scenario and asked him whether, if our positions were reversed and he had come up with my brilliant sub placement, he would show it to me at the end of the game. He said he would. And I called him a big fat liar. He swore he would, and replied that it was a moot point because I would have never asked him to show it to me.

I know it's hard to believe, but this discussion continued in this vein for some time, and only ended after I stuck my tongue out at him, which really offended him for some reason. He ended up leaving the apartment to "get some air" and took our dog on an extended walk.

This is why we hadn't played in so long. (I'm pretty good at not remembering things that I don't want to.) And this is why I was now faced with the possibility of not playing now, or probably ever again, if I refused to give in to my husband's request.

I certainly don't believe that Cosmas had premeditated the whole situation, but I will say I was a bit perturbed by his timing. I mean, couldn't he have mentioned this clause before I had set up my board? (Yes, my two-person sub was already nestled in its secret place.) I briefly entertained just saying yes, because I really did want to play. But I did not want to show him my board if I won. Period.

But I knew that as soon as I said no, that would end my chances of getting to play Battleship by candlelight tonight. It hardly seemed fair that I should be penalized for winning a game before we even started to play. I thought about agreeing to his terms and if by chance I won again by my skilled sub placement, I could always just snag it off the board before I had to show where I had placed it. Granted, this wouldn't be the most mature move on my part, but all is fair in love and Battleship warfare, right?

"I can't believe you." Cosmas was now pissed, and I was pretty sure that being pissed by candlelight was not going to get us in the Romance Hall of Fame.

I had no choice but to respond. I tried the nice-wife approach first. "Why don't we just agree to disagree." I'm not sure where I pulled that load of crap from, but I had to admit that it sounded positive.

"That's the dumbest thing I've ever heard." Okay, maybe it was positively dumb.

"Please, let's just play. Who knows if I'll even win?" This sounded even more insincere on my part because I had a spectacular record of crushing wins when it came to playing games with my husband, and I never go into competitive situations thinking that I won't win. It's not in my nature.

He said I was being lame to make this a big deal. I yelped back that it wasn't me who was making it a big deal, it was he who was being the lame duck, and then I quacked at him.

One of the biggest character flaws I have is lack of control of my big mouth. I used to have control when I was younger, as I never talked back to my parents (well, I did, but they quickly put a stop to it). In fact, people are always assuming that I was the class clown growing up, the wiseass who sat in the back row who had a comment for everything. Nope. I kept my mouth shut then, too. I also sat in the front row. Of course, I was always shouting things in my head—the right answers to questions, cracks about the people who didn't know the answers to questions, etc.—but I never opened my mouth out of turn.

Some might say I had a healthy respect for authority, or others might say I was a chicken who was scared of getting in trouble. I think it was a little of both.

But now—now that I was no longer in school and no longer even working at a standard day job (with a boss who could send me to the unemployment line, which was far worse than the principal's office), I was probably a bit of a nightmare. Any self-regulation mechanism that I had was now idle, and I just went for it every single time. What's worse is that after a lifetime of school and a ten-year graduate program that I like to call "my twenties in Manhattan," I was now equipped with a bigger vocabulary, and the ability to wield my razor-sharp sarcasm skills in a way that would impress Quentin Tarantino.

I mean, what kind of wife quacks at her husband? (I rue-fully wondered if I should have quacked "AFLAC" instead of the regular quack, whether that would have helped.)

My number two flaw was that I wasn't the greatest at apologizing, either. I mean, sure I could say it, but it was hard not to do it with a sardonic smile, which of course only made matters worse.

"Did you just quack at me?"

It's a really bad idea to fight by candlelight because it makes people's eyes flicker in a very menacing way.

I raced through my options—*I sneezed, I coughed, I burped, it was the dog.*

Well, at least I wasn't a sociopath; I knew how to show remorse.

"Maybe." (I suck, why didn't I just say yes? Now I'm gonna get it.)

"So you don't know if you quacked at me?"

I felt like Donald Duck in the principal's office. I wish I could do impressions, because talking like Donald would probably be the only way to salvage this situation.

"Yes, I quacked at you, and it was wrong of me." I took a deep breath, hoping that would stop me from continuing. It didn't. "But I ..."

I watched as Cosmas slowly shut the lid on his game-board command center. He then got up off the bed and walked out of the room.

As bad as having an inane fight by candlelight might have been, being alone by candlelight after an inane fight was definitely worse. I looked down at my five battleships, which I had so carefully placed on the board, and I even pulled off the little sub and stared really hard at it. How absolutely ridiculous that my evening was now ruined over an inch of plastic that was shaped into a submarine. I wondered if real wartime commanders had this problem. Maybe one gets home after a long day of waging war and his wife is in bed reading and she asks him about his day, and he says that it was pretty tiring, but he thought he came up with a brilliant strategy in terms of sub placement. So if the wife, who is a little bored after being alone all day, is a bit curious and asks where he put his ships, would he tell her even though he isn't supposed to? I mean, he probably shouldn't because maybe she is a spy, and then if he divulges the information and she sells it to the enemy, he is putting the lives of his men at risk.

Of course, there were no lives at risk right now. Well, maybe just mine if I wanted to stay married. I thought about putting my sub back on the board and walking into the living room and just handing over my entire control panel; yes, maybe that's what was needed, a grand gesture on my part. As I started to put my little sub back in its hiding place I hesitated, and I wondered whether it would be totally evil of me to place it back in a different space, because, after all, why did I have to show him where I really put my sub if I didn't want to? I had certainly read the rules and there was no discussion of the winner having to divulge her fleet after the fact.

Fine, it was wrong to quack at him. And maybe it is impolite to talk trash at your husband by candlelight. But was it so wrong to stand up for myself when it came to my own beliefs about fair game play? I mean, why was it that I had to be the one to give in? As dorky as it sounded, why couldn't we agree to disagree? And, sure, I have a few flaws (okay, I have lots), but it's not like I'm married to a saint (even if he was named after one). What about the fact that he is stubborn too? What about the fact that he never wants to play board games with me, even when I promise to be on my best behavior? Sure, I'm a bigger fan of game playing than he is, but so what? Maybe he should suck it up and play more often, because God knows I have always gamely gone into every freakin' antiques store that we happen to pass by. I suck it up and look at overpriced old stuff that I can't help wonder if it was so great why it's now for sale, so why can't he play a few games with me even if he doesn't find it all that fun? (Let me say, however, that by winning I'm usually in a really good mood, if you know what I mean. So it's not like he doesn't benefit too.)

It was then that Cosmas appeared in the doorway. He was obviously taking the high road here and it was now up to me to meet him halfway.

"I am woman, hear me quack?" I offered uncertainly, half-knowing that I had sunk my chances of ever playing Battleship again.

Oh well, maybe you can't win them all.

SHE SCORES

I'm not the type to really believe that all the head trips we have as adults can be traced back to our youth. I just don't buy it, because the idea seems like a bit of a cop-out to me. "I didn't get the job because I did not get hugged enough as a child." I mean that just sounds ridiculous, right? But lately I've been wondering whether there is more truth to this idea than I care to admit (I am a chronic procrastinator because I was not hugged enough as a child?).

My parents moved to the U.S. from Korea in their late twenties, arriving with two large fake-leather suitcases, a baby (my older sister, Helen), and my father's medical degree. After a stint in New York State, they eventually settled in Tennessee (my dad was into land and trees), so my older brother, John, and I were both born in Nashville, Tennessee. At the time there were very few Asian families living in Tennessee, so I was raised to be far more American than Korean. In fact, I personally have very little allegiance to Korea at all, since I don't speak or even understand the language, and in fact have only visited once, when I was eight (and my most vivid memory of the trip was that the hotel where we stayed had this fabulous bakery in the lobby that made these really yummy twisty doughnuts—nice, huh?).

It's not that I'm disassociating myself from my parents or even my heritage, but everything you need to know about me is pretty much based on the fact that I was born and raised in America, and damn proud of it, if you want to know the truth. From the outside, it would appear that I had a pretty typical 1970s/'80s childhood filled with McDonald's, Tang, Cap'n Crunch cereal, Smurfs, *Dallas,* roller-skating birthday parties, *Footloose,* and a big crush on George Michael.

But where my "typical" childhood took a dramatic left turn was in the home, where I was raised in a very Asian way. So like most of my Asian-American peers, I had parents who weren't just strict about education, they were totally obsessed with it (I knew all the Ivy League schools before I could write cursive), and I'm starting to realize that it was through this upbringing that I developed the foundation of my personality. I was brought up to be goal oriented, and maybe that sounds like a pretty positive thing to be, certainly useful in a society that prizes achievement, but like all character traits, it has its drawbacks as well.

Being goal oriented when young was probably a good thing, because it gave me something to focus my high energy into. (If ADHD were known about in the '70s I would have most certainly been a prime candidate for Ritalin or Adderall.) So where my mother didn't have access to a pill to keep me in line, she used fear first, and if that didn't bring about the desired results, she had no qualms offering bribes.

In Sunday school we were once given an assignment to memorize Bible verses, and for every ten Bible verses you memorized you would receive a biblical bookmark (it was probably frowned upon to give out cash), and there was even a chart that was hung in the hallway next to the restrooms that listed the ranking of how many bookmarks each child had earned. Now, in case you don't have many Asian friends, let me just say that there is nothing that an Asian loves more than a ranking system.

I was never once told that I should just do my best and that that would be good enough; no, I was told that I had to do my best and I damn well better place in the top three. So when I came out of the restroom one Sunday and found my mom standing in front of the chart, I knew that when she turned around her eyes would be gleaming in a way I would find a little frightening. Of course, I then snuck out the back entrance, where minutes later she found me leaning up against the car admiring my most recent laminated bookmark, trying to avoid all eye contact. You see, I was pretty satisfied with my small and growing collection of bookmarks and my middle-of-the-chart rankings (wasn't pride a sin?), but my mother, well, she had something else in mind.

Luckily, I did not grow up in a household where sugar cereals were forbidden, but my mother had come to the conclusion that candy caused cavities, so she was a bit stingy in the candy department, which probably wasn't such a bad thing, as I really didn't need the extra sugar energy. Yes, candy was pretty scarce back then, which only made it that much more attractive. Candy was king and quickly became currency in our household, used only for special things (everyday things like making my bed or picking up my room did not get me candy, that was just something that I had to do, like breathing). No, candy was the big gun.

My two favorite candies—or perhaps they became my favorites because that's what my mom bought, and beggars can't be choosers—were Kraft caramels and lemon drops. She bought them in big bags, which she wisely kept hidden away in her bedroom. (We were never allowed in our parents' room unless they were in there, and when we were invited to join them it was usually not a good thing.)

So there I was on the following Saturday afternoon, sitting at the kitchen table swinging my legs and staring out the window instead of memorizing Bible verses like I was supposed to. I was desperate to go outside and play, but I knew it wouldn't be a possibility until after "homework time." (I had to spend two hours a day, every day, sitting at the kitchen table doing homework—whether I had any or not.) This is when I heard her bedroom door open, which was followed by the quick clicking of my mom's house slippers on the wall-to-wall carpeting; she was coming my way. Like the chicken I was, I immediately crouched over my book and did my best to scrunch up my face as if I were having the words physically seared into my brain. I didn't even look up when she entered the room, so great was my pretend dedication to my task at hand.

As I stared hard at the flash cards I had made with index cards (my mom was very pro-flash cards), something showed up in my peripheral vision—something small, square, light brown, and wrapped in cellophane. Yes, it was a Kraft caramel and it was being pushed across the table by one of my mom's brightly lacquered red nails. I didn't dare reach out for it (fear of the brightly lacquered red nails), because I knew that these were things that were never doled out to show random affection; no, these little squares meant business.

Without taking my eyes off the prize, I said in a very heartfelt, but very calm manner, "I'll do anything." Obviously, I lacked the ability to play it cool.

I looked up at my mother, who was smiling with the power she held over me, and I couldn't help but smile back, because I was already imagining the glee of holding the little treasure in my hand, and also because I was nervous as hell.

It was then that she asked me where I was on the chart, and I knew this was just showmanship on her part, as I had witnessed her memorizing the chart six days previously, but I played along. I said that I was sixth or seventh out of twenty kids, and I let her correct me by telling me that I was eighth out of twenty-one. It was obvious what she was leading up to, and I didn't even blink an eye, because if she wanted me at the top of the chart badly enough to offer up candy, then her wish was my command.

We then sat down together to strategize my ascent, and we decided that I could nail the top slot in two Sundays, and my reign could continue for at least another week or two until the end of the month. We figured out how much "homework time" it would take, who were my main competitors, and lastly, we came up with a price. I would get one caramel now just for incentive. I would get one more tomorrow if I hit my first goal, and I would get the last three when I hit the top of the chart. (And for every week that I could hold my number one position I would get one, if not two, more, depending on how generous she was feeling, and also whether I was also showing proper dental care.)

It was then that I became a master negotiator, because I wanted to know what second place would get me. First place was currently being held by a little brainiac with huge glasses whose claim to fame was that all three of his namesakes were apostles. Luke John Mark (or was it Peter Luke Mark?) was the kid that you almost felt sorry for due to his lack of friends and a social life, outside of his very religious parents, well, until he started to walk back to his seat from the front of the classroom with that smug little holier-than-thou look upon his face.

I was informed that since this was not a true academic achievement, second place would just get me that much closer to God, and that maybe I could ask him for candy. Talk about playing hardball.

And poof, she was gone, just like that, and the only proof

that our conversation even happened was now stuck to the roof of my mouth and rapidly dissolving. After a few minutes of strong tongue work I was left with only a memory of buttery sweetness and the promise of more to come.

Over the next few hours a parade of clowns could have passed by the window, and I would have never known. I was now a girl with a goal. Even though we had decided that I should probably go easy and only shoot for two bookmarks on the following day, I decided that I needed to make a bigger showing and try for three. I knew the only way to do this with one day's notice was to nail the short ones first, leaving the longer, wordier biblical passages for the following week, as I would then be even more motivated by being within striking distance of my goal. So I divided up my flash cards according to number of words per verse and hunkered down.

The next morning I raised my hand to go first, and as I went through my first ten with lightning speed, I could hear my bored classmates whispering amongst themselves. After receiving my first bookmark, I politely informed my teacher that I would like to go on, and with this announcement I garnered a bit more attention. I kicked butt on the second set, and when I collected my second bookmark I leaned in and whispered to my teacher that, again, I wanted to continue. No one had ever attempted more than twenty verses at a time—well, besides Matthew Paul Mark, but that was to be expected. With all eyes on me, I did not grow more nervous, but instead grew bolder and more self-assured. After all, I had stayed up well past my bedtime sitting in my closet, using its light to shuffle through my flash cards. I got a hearty round of applause when I received my third bookmark, and a promise from the teacher that after class I could accompany her to the chart, where she would reorder the rankings.

After the main worship service had finished, I brought my mother to the chart and showed her how I had moved up five slots to number three, and though I could tell she was pleased, she kept her praise light and warned me that I should be humble. In the car ride home I remember getting a little sullen over my mom's cool reception of the fact that I had memorized and recited thirty Bible verses, which was ten more than the goal we had set together for me. I was doing that bratty-kid thing where I was petulantly pressing my face against the window (which she hated, as I made smudges on the glass) while sighing every ten seconds. She put a stop to my bad mood by tossing a lemon drop into my lap (she kept a few in her change purse for emergency purposes), and after picking off some lint, I was back on track.

Eventually, the bribes changed to cold cash for every A, though it was always kept interesting because one B would get me nothing. And from cash it went to material objects like designer handbags and new shoes, and I soon became a grown-up who was totally motivated by consumer goods and little else. Sure I was satisfied with a job well done, but at the same time I learned how to reward myself, sometimes with small things like a fatty forbidden Frappuccino and sometimes with big things like a new scarf or a pair of designer sunglasses. I was well aware of the vicious cycle my life had become and I would sometimes try to forgo the reward system, but it was of little use, since I was basically a human version of Pavlov's dog, someone who began to salivate as soon as she entered Bergdorf Goodman.

And now? Now I was in my thirties and realizing that there was probably more to life than a new iPod, new purse, or even (gasp) new shoes. Sure I still had goals—lose weight, write a novel, write a screenplay, break my bad habit of procrastinating—but they were the same goals I'd had for a while and there wasn't much progress on them. Why was it that I could find no satisfaction by simply just doing things? Why did there always have to be a carrot at the end of a stick before I could move forward? Not that I would really do anything for one lousy carrot, well, unless we were talking about diamond carats.

I know there are worse things to be than obsessively goal oriented, but sometimes I found my whole mentality a little tiring. It takes a lot of energy to always come up with material objects that I want, and many times after reaching my goal and getting my prize I wouldn't even be all that happy with whatever I had won. It was more that I just liked the thrill of the chase, and I guess I should be thankful that I wasn't born a good-looking guy, because I would most certainly be labeled a cad.

I suppose that I have reached an age where I want to be more than just a woman with a lot of stuff. Sure I love all my stuff, but this feeling I have of always wanting more isn't going to be filled by only material goods. I hope I am not that woman who will never be satisfied with what she has, but rather that I will be the woman who realizes she has a lot, and can learn to offer others more. Perhaps it's time to set myself some new goals for what type of person I want to be in my future. Obviously, I'd like to be a woman who has nice things, but I'd like to be more than that, too. Sometimes I wish that my parents had told me from time to time that I should just do my best and it would be just fine, or perhaps had even doled out a little more candy and hugs for no reason at all, but I know they did it because they just wanted what was best for me. It was now my turn to figure out what that best actually meant.

I never did make it to the top of the Bible-verse chart. I put in a really strong showing the following week by memorizing another thirty Bible verses (some of which were quite long), but John Peter Luke had recited forty, breaking a classroom record (and impressing even me), so he retained his top-of-the-chart status. My mom was true to her word and I did not receive any more Kraft caramels, but I did receive a second-place ribbon, which I saved with the hope that I could trade it in for candy at a later date.

THE PIMPLE
THAT CAME TO DINNER

As a teenager you believed that everything was going to ruin your life. If your mom wouldn't buy you a pair of the latest and greatest Nike cross trainers, your life was essentially over. If you couldn't find your Bonne Bell purple-plum Lip Smackers gloss, then you might as well jump out the window. If you didn't get an A in math, then you'd be grounded and you'd miss Mary Kay's thirteenth-birthday party at the roller-skating rink (where her hunky older brother Steve, who was a SENIOR, would be chaperoning with his friends instead of her parents, so basically you and your friends would be able to do anything you wanted without fear of parental recourse), and if that happened then you might as well just lie down on the train tracks and wait for your ruined freakin' life to be over already.

Of course, one of the biggest ways that your life could get ruined in your teenage years was the ongoing battle with pimples. Sure, everyone else was suffering from them too, except for those few lucky girls blessed with good genes (we hated them), and the ones who had really nice moms who would actually let them call in sick to school when they had a pimple, rather than have to suffer the humiliation of going to school and being called "crater face" (we hated their mothers); but you were still immature enough that you only really worried about yourself.

But somehow you survived (barely), and in your twenties you were making your own income and were happy to blow all your cash on copayments to the dermatologist and on overpriced skin-care systems that promised you a face like a supermodel's if only you followed seven steps every morning and every night for the rest of your life (or at least until you were broke). And sure enough, you finally reached the age where pimples were no longer a problem, and you thought hallelujah, your true life could now really begin. Now you could really see what it was like to have supermodel-clear skin while perched on some craggy cliff, staring broodingly out into the crashing waves, just like in those moody black-and-white ad campaigns where it's hard to pinpoint precisely the product they are pushing. Phew.

So when you hit your thirties and your skin gets all blotchy again, you now know that your teenage years were nothing to complain about (I mean, c'mon, you were lucky enough to have the metabolism of a racehorse back then and you could actually eat an entire bag of Cheetos without much more consequence than having orange fingertips for a few hours). Because having pimples, or even a single shining one, was enough to really ruin your world, this time thirty-something style.

Angst as a teenager is certainly horrible, and it's really a shame how many hours you wasted locked in your room staring into a hand mirror while talking on the phone to your best friend and giving her a play-by-play on your face *(Ew. It's still there. Will you talk to me at school on Monday even if it's not gone?)*, but you were young and you had plenty of free time, since the mall wasn't open twenty-four hours back then. But angst as you get older is far worse, not only because you no longer have as much free time in which to lock yourself in your room and obsess with a hand mirror (and, if you did, you'd be on your own because all your close female friends are probably too busy to spend an hour on the phone talking about the injustice of acne in your thirties), but also because you are supposed to be old enough to know that having a very prominent red pimple the size of an SUV parked front and center on your left cheek won't *really* result in the ruination of your life. Right.

But what happens when you're trapped in a car in the middle of a six-hour road trip, where all you have is time to stare at your face and wonder whether in fact your latest indignity is the size of a Hummer or just a Chevy Suburban? And right when you're convinced that it is indeed still growing before your eyes, your husband reaches over and snaps the visor shut. You jerk your head backward in fear of getting clipped by the visor, since you now have lost all judgment on the size of your face because you basically feel as if you've got a second head growing out of your left cheek.

Of course, you scowl at him for this, though it's not like that required any effort because you've been scowling for two days straight anyway, ever since the onset of the volcano now emerging from the surface of your face. Without a word, you pull the mirror back down, and are momentarily shocked again to see your once familiar face blurred in the background of the angry red bump that appears to be pulsing with a heartbeat all its own. Your husband, stupidly, tries to close the mirror again, but this time you're ready for him and your left hand shoots out and grabs him by the wrist in midair. You are both surprised by how strong you are and you briefly wonder if perhaps you are actually bionic and if this is the case then maybe you now have a bionic zit on your face (able to shoot pus with such force that you could kill someone).

He tries to pull his hand free, as he does need it to drive, and though you know you should let it go, you also can't help but contemplate that one swift jerk and the car would go careening off the highway, resulting in the fiery death of your zit once and for all. But then you think about the coroner who'd be assigned to do your autopsy and the fact that he would probably cluck his tongue and feel sorry for the funeral parlor makeup artist who is going to have a doozy of a time covering this zit on your face (knowing your luck, it

will be the only part of your body that didn't get burned beyond recognition). It is this very thought that makes you realize you have really sunk as far as you could go in that
ocean known as self-pity and shameful vanity.

You let go of his arm, and then go back to looking in the
mirror.

"You are driving me crazy with this. Seriously, can you
give it a rest?"

Men. Sure we share the planet with them, and in some
ways we need them, but when it comes down to it, we are
nothing alike.

You explain to him that you've been so busy dealing with
getting ready for the Thanksgiving road trip to Philly to see
your family, that you really haven't had the time to give this
pimple its fair homage. Obviously, it was making some sort
of grand statement by showing up at all, and now it is really
angry after being ignored for two days. Everyone knows
that an unwatched pimple goes on boiling. Like a tick, it
uses your own body against you to grow ever fatter. Sad,
but true. After all, you're an expert, seeing that you've now
been studying them for the last twenty freakin' years.

This is when he tells you that it's "*barely* noticeable," and
that your face will be back to normal by next week. Next
week? NEXT WEEK? So is he saying that you're going to
have to live like this for another five to seven days?

Thanks for visiting denial land (a nice place to live), and
welcome to the state of utter horror!

Oh God, maybe he's right. Because you're certain that it

is still in the developing stage, which means at least another forty-eight hours before you can pop it (we all know that popping a zit too soon only leads to an extra three days), and then it will probably take another three or four days for your face to recover from the trauma of it all. He's right, it's going to be at least a week, at the minimum, and to make matters worse, you're going to have to spend five of those days in the company of a camera-happy family! Like you really need a thirty-third set of Thanksgiving pictures anyway. *Smile, you've just consumed four thousand calories and it's not even four o'clock! Hey everyone, Jenny cooked up one big pimple—I mean, turkey....*

Suddenly, you're desperate to turn around and head back home. If only you could just crawl in bed with a tube of Clearasil and a few magazines (a necessary evil that would help pass the time, but also make you feel even worse about it all [damn! I need some airbrushing]) and just wait it out. If only you could pull over and find some seedy highway motel where everyone has much bigger things to worry about than the girl in Room 810 who won't even leave her room to get maid service. If only you could pit-stop in New York and find the home address of your one great dermatologist and crash her own Thanksgiving (peopled by her own brilliantly clear-skinned family), promising to send all of your pimply-faced future children to her as future patients. If only you were a rap star whose gimmick was wearing a Band-Aid on your face that you could move around whenever you had a pimple. If only. If only. If only.

Okay, cue the orchestral score, because here comes the lecture. Because, since you're no longer fifteen, but quite a *few* years older than that (eighteen years older, but who's counting?), you should really be mature enough to know that the holidays are not the time to be spent thinking of your own vanity and wishing you were a criminal who could wear a ski mask all the time. The holidays are a time when you should just be happy that you have your health and are fortunate to spend a little time with your family, blah blah blah. This is one of the biggest drags of being older—that you now have the ability—nay, responsibility—of looking at the big picture, at the world around yourself, realizing that there are plenty of people far worse off than you who would probably be happy to suffer the humiliation of a giant mountain on their face (make it two) to have the life that you have. (After all, you have a kickin' new cell phone that allows you to download all these fun, groovy ring tones!)

So before your husband gets through the opening of his you-are-really-being-a-diva-and-I-mean-that-in-a-bad-way-as-opposed-to-a-cute-sardonic-T-shirt-way, you stop him and say you don't need to hear about Plymouth Rock and everything, as you already have one on your face and you promise not to mention it again, which you then punctuate by snapping the visor mirror shut of your own volition. So there, is he happy now, Mr. The-Only-Blemishes-I-Get-These-Days-Are-Usually-Hidden-By-My-Beard? You hope so, because right now you're actually feeling that the life of being the bearded lady in a carnival sideshow might not be so bad, after all. You've always wanted to travel the country more, and you've always been a fan of sequins....

You even manage to forget about the pimple for a while by turning your attention to the fact that you and your husband are on your way to see your brother and his wife, who have just had their first child (pregnancy being the only time when there is any good that can come out of a large bump taking shape on one's body). Luckily for everyone involved, the baby is a boy (Benjamin), so he is protected from growing up to be a teenage girl who must spend her entire youth in fear of waking up every day to find something unwanted staring back in her pink Hello Kitty hand mirror that she has bought at the mall. Thinking about your new nephew even makes you come close to smiling, as you think about his brand-new life with his brand-new ten fingers and toes, all of which have come complete with brand-new supercollagenized skin that is so soft that you finally get the whole soft-as-a-baby's-bottom comment.

How great to be able to have a whole life ahead of you with all the joyful fun of being a kid—you know, the new Big Wheel, learning how to ride a bicycle, and finding out that you passed your driving test even though you almost ran a stoplight but didn't and then said a really vulgar word—and perhaps it's these things that one should focus on, as opposed to some of life's smaller and uglier bumps. Sure, you are living with a cruise ship docked on your face right now, but with any luck, in a week's time, the ship will set sail (hopefully not to another part of your face—you hope it freakin' sinks) and you will have forgotten all about it. And, really, would you honestly trade all the things you are thankful for in your life just to get rid of the skyscraper shooting off your face?

It's probably wrong to let small things ruin your entire Thanksgiving. But then, dammit, it's also wrong that you still get zits when you're old enough to understand this. So now you only have a hundred miles to go until you get to Philly, and you'll soon get your first glimpse of your new nephew, baby Ben, which may make you even happier than the fact that you'll also have access to a much larger mirror, and a lock on the door.

MOTHER'S MILK

It has been said that it takes the brain twenty minutes to register that you have eaten food and have in fact satiated your hunger. So the theory is that if you eat just a little, say maybe half of what you normally eat, and then stop and wait twenty minutes, you will probably feel totally satisfied. (Please note the word "probably.")

Okay, this certainly sounds reasonable, but one of the problems with this theory is that many of us don't wait until we are hungry to eat. No, many of us (and I won't name names) actually think about eating as soon as we get up in the morning, before we are even awake enough to know whether we are hungry; and then we continue to fantasize about food throughout the rest of the day, until we go to sleep at night and dream about pancakes. (I'm of course doing the low-carb thing lately, and I can honestly say that I don't really miss bread all that much, and even though I do miss pasta, I'm not despondent without it, but I am broken-hearted over my breakup with pancakes. *My name is Jenny, and it's been over 165 days since my last pancake.*)

My mother really brought the whole thing to my attention for me. She said, and I quote, "Do you want to know what your problem is?" She didn't wait for my answer; because, of course, it wasn't really a question but more of a preview of the coming attraction of Mother and Daughter Spar XVII.

"You think about food too much. That's why you're …"— she pauses here, searching for the right word—"heavy now." By "now" she means for the past four years since I've been married, which is when I may or may not have put on about twenty pounds. "I don't blame you totally. …" This is nice of her, that my own mom isn't blaming me totally for my own weight gain. Though I know she certainly isn't going to blame herself (even though I'm willing to toss some of the blame in her direction, since she's the one who's been commenting on what I eat since, oh, I was born), so I'm curious to hear what she says. "It's *his* fault too." At this, I picture her looking down at her perfectly manicured nails, to show remorse that she had to cast a single stone at my husband, Cosmas, whom she normally finds to be a paragon of perfection. (I'm sure it's annoying when your mother doesn't like your husband, but let me say that having your mother like your husband more than she likes you is no picnic either.)

As much as I despise talking about my weight with my mother (akin to how I might despise having shards of glass jabbed into my eyes), I decide that I am willing to listen to her latest theory about my weight. Sometimes I think I should save myself some time and stop obsessing about my weight, mainly because my mother does such a good job of it on her own. I say, "Go on," which is all I am willing to give at this point in time, not that it matters, because I know she's going to tell me her thoughts whether I offer encouragement or not.

"Cosmas has such good taste and such a love for fine things, like good food, and it's natural that his healthy appetite might affect you negatively. But"—did you ever doubt there would be a but?—"*you* need to forget about good food. Leave the good food for him." Only my mom can turn a negative and make it into a positive, at least when it comes to Cosmas. "Don't ever eat dessert. Desserts are bad." She continues on and I decide that it's time to stop her before she starts listing every other food group that is bad for me too.

"Mom. I get it."

She either doesn't hear me or, more likely, she hears me but keeps going because I'm being rude by interrupting and I now need to be punished by having to listen to her rattle off a few more things that I should never ever eat again. Things like potato chips, candy, popcorn at movies; in fact, no snacks at all. Snacks are bad. She tells me that I should eat more fish and lean meats, broccoli, and spinach.

And then I have to hear for the one millionth time how as

a baby I did not like any green baby food, and would always spit it out, and so, afraid that I would starve, she mainly fed me my favorite baby food, which was banana, and if only she would have known that hooking me on carbs would lead me to thirty-three years later being "heavy," then she would have surely made me eat my vegetables. But still, she's not blaming herself; she's just giving me all the facts.

By this time I am not even holding the phone to my ear anymore, as I am so annoyed at myself for falling for this bait-and-switch routine of hers. I thought she was going to let Cosmas be the subject of her critical eye for a change, but she had fooled me again and only used him as bait to get me to stay on the phone, so I could hear the same old how-and-why-Jenny-needs-to-lose-weight lecture once again. Same story. Different day. Though this time I am going to stop her before she turns it into a double feature—the one where she laments to me about the fact that my older brother, John, is too skinny (big dramatic Mom sigh), and if only he had a healthy appetite like mine, she wouldn't have to worry so much (big dramatic Mom sigh number two). No, if John were a good eater like me, then she would be so happy. Tsk. Tsk. She just can't believe how he always forgets to eat, and my, my how different her two children happen to be. (Insert fake laughter, because she's really not amused, since she'd rather we be more similar, me being more like John.)

I finally manage to get off the phone by banging my head against the wall and telling her that I have to go because someone is knocking. She's suspicious, of course, because it seems like I get an awful lot of visitors when we're on the phone, and then she warns me that it better not be the pizza-delivery guy, in case I didn't hear her before, because "Pizza is bad. Don't ever eat pizza." Just once, I wish I had the nerve to tell her it was indeed the pizza guy at my door who was bringing me a large, fattening pizza that I was going to eat all by myself. (Childish, I know, but of course I never had the nerve to say it, and if I did, she'd probably hop on the next plane and show up in person to find the pizza-delivery guy and bribe him to never darken my doorstep again.)

It's probably safe to assume that most mothers and daughters have some ongoing issue between them, and I suppose there are worse things we could fight about, but what's disheartening about our interaction is that it hasn't really changed in the last two decades. I have very clear rec-ollections of having similar conversations with my mom when she was driving me to the mall and Madonna's "Lucky Star" was playing on the radio. She was warning me to keep my distance from the food court, and I was staring out the window wondering whether they sold new moms at the mall.

I mean, perhaps it's time that my mother and I find something else to talk about besides food. I am willing to concede that she does have a point and that I am probably guilty of spending too much time thinking about food on a daily basis (though these days it's more thinking about what

I can't eat, versus what I am going to eat), but obviously it doesn't help that every time I get on the phone with her she brings it up too. Sample conversation:

Me: *Hi, Mom.*

Mom: *I got tired of waiting for you to call, so I'm calling you.*

Me: *I was going to call you later today.*

Mom: *That's nice. It's nice when a daughter calls her mother.*

Me: *So what's new with you?*

Mom: *What do you mean? My life is the same every day.*

Me: *(in my head)* Then why do we need to talk so often?

Me: *(for real) Okay, Mom, whatever you say.*

Mom: *What did you eat for lunch today? (Or, depending on the time of day, you can substitute "breakfast" or "dinner" for "lunch.")*

And this is the point where I would outright lie and say that I had a salad for lunch, or a salad for dinner, and that I didn't eat breakfast because I never eat breakfast and I just don't understand why she always asks what I have for breakfast AFTER I'VE TOLD HER A THOUSAND TIMES THAT I NEVER EVER EAT BREAKFAST! In fact, I wish she would call me on my lie one day and just say, "You are totally full of crap, because if you ate salads as much as you say you do, then I wouldn't have to worry about your weight." At which point I would say, "You're right, Mother, I am full of crap, and you know what? I never eat salads at home, because I hate to make them. I hate washing lettuce. I hate drying lettuce [I don't like wet lettuce in salads]. I hate chopping up vegetables to put in the salad so that it doesn't look like I'm only eating lettuce."

I would then get in trouble for saying the word "crap," which isn't fair because she used it first, but I would be slightly chagrined for yelling at my mother. (Obviously, I have no problems with lying to her, but yelling is worse. I lie in self-defense.)

She would then tell me that it's not nice to lie to one's mother. And I would say that it's not nice to pick on one's daughter. She would deny picking on me. I would give her fourteen million examples of it. She would be silent like a stone. I would be exhilarated but also scared to death. She would then use the universal Mom defense, which is that she was only "commenting" on my weight because she was trying to be helpful. (Geez, whatever happened to the good old days of food as love?) This is where I would lose it and start to get shrill. HELPFUL? YOU THINK IT'S HELPFUL FOR ME TO HAVE YOU RIDING ME ABOUT MY WEIGHT EVERY SINGLE TIME WE TALK? AND YOU WONDER WHY I DON'T EVER CALL YOU. ARE YOU FOR REAL?

Sarcasm never goes over so well with my mother, and the combo of yelling at her and being sarcastic is going to put me in enough hot water that I could be served as a new drink at Starbucks—one venti guilt latte, coming right up.

My mom, God love her, is the master of the sad-mom-martyr voice; Meryl Streep could take lessons from her. "Sometimes I think you don't call me because you are having too much fun and just forget about me." *(I swear, Meryl, she actually says stuff like this.)*

Her performance is so moving that I almost want to take out my violin and play a song for her. She's a one-woman opera.

According to my watch, it's been twenty minutes and my brain has just registered that it's totally and completely useless to try to resolve this issue with my mom. It just can't be done. Even if I ever had the courage to confront her for real, I know that it would always end up with me in the wrong. It's wrong to lie to your mom. It's wrong of moms to pick on their daughters about their weight. It's wrong to yell at your mom. It's wrong that moms always can escape any confrontation by using the guilt expressway.

I decide that it's time to make amends with pancakes. Instead of making a whole batch, I do the math and make just one, which I plan to eat very slowly. Maybe I'll even call my mom after I eat it, while I'm waiting for my brain to catch up. Hell, I'll shake up her world and tell her that I had breakfast. She'll then ask me what I had. And I'll say, "A salad, obviously." Sighing for good measure. "Pancakes are bad, you know that."

OOPS, I COULDN'T DO IT

I don't have very much in common with Britney Spears. I am not blond; I am not a multimillionaire; I am not in my early twenties; I cannot sing (I am that woman who makes others cringe during karaoke); I cannot dance (well, I can, but more like Molly Ringwald in *The Breakfast Club*); I do not have big bodyguards; I am not followed at all times by paparazzi; and I certainly wouldn't have gotten married so young (and so often), if I were Britney.

What I *will* say is that I find it kind of sad that I actually know so much about her. She drinks a lot of Red Bull; she likes hats; she likes short shorts; she smokes Marlboro Lights; she gave her mom a Mercedes for her birthday; she's from Louisiana; she likes to shop (but honestly, what multi-millionaire doesn't?); and, perhaps most of all, she likes the color pink.

Now, granted, I think she's made a few missteps lately when it comes to her love life and her career, but I'm not here to criticize her, or to make fun of her, or to offer up advice. In fact, I'll even own up to being a fan (not an avid fan, mind you; I mean, it's not like I write her letters, put her posters on my walls, or long to meet her, or anything), but I have bought a few of her albums, and sung along in the car (I've always been a Top 40 girl, no matter how uncool that is), and I've certainly commented on all of her fashion faux pas along with everyone else.

But what I want to praise her for are two things. One, it's obvious that she likes to eat junk food (she's been photographed with Cheetos and Doritos more than once), and I find this oddly comforting, because it's easy to imagine that all the starlets in Hollywood are probably hungry enough to eat their own arms if they were ever left alone long enough to do so. So good for Brit that she is a woman who knows what she likes (processed cheese, obviously) and does not deny herself. And why should she, when she obviously also works out so much (though she has been getting chunky lately, which is not to say chunky like I'm chunky, but rather chunky for a star, which is a totally different scale—and by the way, yes I *do* feel I'm within my rights to comment on celebrities' waistlines, because—hey—they make lots of money, have personal trainers, and receive lots of free shoes, so it's only fair).

But what I find absolutely amazing is that I saw her interviewed on *The Ellen DeGeneres Show* once, and Ellen casually asked her about her famous stomach (I mean, does this girl even *own* a shirt that covers her belly? Lord help us now that she's knocked up, as I'm sure the tabloids will find a way to show us her blossoming belly in 3-D), and they got into a discussion of doing sit-ups, or "crunches" as they are called now, and Britney said that she did five hundred sit-ups a day, well sometimes she did one thousand, but she always did at least five hundred. (I'm just going to ignore the whole one thousand part, really, it's just too much to comprehend.)

THAT'S RIGHT. FIVE HUNDRED SIT-UPS A DAY. EVERY DAY.

Ellen's eyes almost popped out of her head, and I'm sure she was thinking, *Your stomach looks good, but not that good.* Five hundred SIT-UPS A DAY. EVERY DAY.

I was equally stunned. Five hundred SIT-UPS A DAY. EVERY DAY is sort of one of those things like the notion of infinite space that a normal person really has a hard time processing. I mean, if she really did five hundred SIT-UPS A DAY. EVERY DAY, how is it that she had any time left over to get herself in so much trouble all the time?

Well, if she or anyone does five hundred SIT-UPS A DAY. EVERY DAY (I mean, besides guys in prison, who, after all, don't have much else to do), I have to say, they *deserve* every million they make. I mean, talk about work.

So then I'm thinking of all the things that a hundred million could buy, and I decide to see whether or not *I* can do five hundred SIT-UPS (though not EVERY DAY, as I'm not stupid). I mean, sure she's younger, stronger, leaner, and blonder than me. But hey, I have nothing else to do, as I've just finished reading my latest *Us Weekly*.

1–10—Wow. Maybe I should look into opening an off-shore bank account.

11–20—I'm still feeling surprisingly good, though perhaps the sugar burst from that Kit Kat I just ate was helping me out.

21–30—I'm feeling a bit of a twinge in my abdominal region.

31–40—The twinge has morphed into a fiery ball of heat.

41–50—Did I say fiery ball? I meant searing, flaming pain.

51–60—I'm trying to lick off any remnants of Kit Kat bar on my lips because I fear these will be my last minutes on Earth. I cross off "open Swiss bank account" on my mental to-do list.

61–63—I topple over at number sixty-three and I am now curled into a fetal position on my right side. There is a piece of rug fuzz that is tickling my nose and will probably be shortly sucked up into it, as I'm breathing quite hard. I do not uncurl my legs, as I'm sure that all the strain has pushed one of my organs through my skin and it will just fall on my rug once I move and then it will get those yucky little hairs all over it, which probably wouldn't be the best thing as I don't know if they have those lint-roll-brush thingies on a standard surgical-instrument tray.

After five minutes the ache has subsided and I think about whether I should even resume this absurd quest, or whether I should get up and go celebrate the fact that I just did sixty-three sit-ups with some ice cream.

I roll back onto my back and decide to keep going.

63–70—My, my, it's surprising how fast searing pain can return.

71–80—I'm pretending I'm Sarah Connor from *Terminator 2* when she's still in the asylum—I mean, talk about a woman who managed to look hot in sweatpants.

81–90—I'm wondering if it is possible to burst a blood vessel in your brain while trying to do this many sit-ups when you're neither rich nor famous nor twenty-something.

91–94—I taste salt and I'm debating whether this is just sweat, or maybe tears mixed in as well.

95–100—I'm not sure if these would any longer even pass for sit-ups, as I can barely pull myself up straight and am now veering off to the sides. . . . I'm even using my hands to try to pull myself up. Once I found a great pair of leather pants on sale and against my better judgment I tried them on. Being stretched out on the floor of a dressing room trying to squirm into leather was really not exactly a highlight Kodak moment in my life; and neither is this.

I am now lying flat on my back, legs outstretched, and I am gasping and groaning and wondering if this is what childbirth feels like. I also wondered whether you had to be pregnant to get an epidural.

I'm not sure how many minutes have passed, but I am

now staring at the ceiling, which I can finally see clearly again, as all the little stars and colored dots that were flashing before my eyes are now gone. Yep. It's just me, the ceiling, and four hundred more to go....

There is no way that I can possibly continue this endeavor without some water and maybe some more chocolate, so I slowly manage to get myself into a standing position. I check my watch, though it does no good, since I can't even remember when I started. But if I had to guess, I'd say I probably lost roughly an hour of my life. On my way over to the fridge, I make a pit stop in front of the full-length mirror hanging on the inside door of the closet in my kitchen to see if my stomach looks any different.

Nada. I repeat, negative.

Two hours later, I'm back on the floor, but not a whole lot has happened since I last managed to get up. I've spent all of this time drinking water, foraging unsuccessfully for more chocolate, checking E-mail, walking my dog to get more chocolate, and, finally, watching part of a *CSI* episode on TiVo. And it was halfway through the show that it occurred to me that perhaps if I continued my sit-ups while watching TV, the next four hundred would go faster. So...

101–120—I only manage to do twenty sit-ups during the last half hour of the show, as I become too engrossed in the case at hand and keep stopping to watch. Obviously, watching TV and sit-ups don't mix as well as, say, TV and Cheetos.

121–140—Hey, these were not so bad, perhaps I'm hitting some sort of groove.

141–150—I begin a debate with myself on whether being over thirty is simply too old to wear those belly-baring shirts.

151–170—Painful, but not crazy painful. I have now decided that I probably couldn't get away with a half-shirt or anything, but if by chance I were to suddenly have a nice flat stomach I could perhaps show off an inch of my midriff from time to time, sort of more like, *Oops, did my shirt ride up again?*

171–180—Clenched teeth.

181–190—Wendell, my dog, starts to bark at me. All of my grunting must be confusing him, or maybe I'm just annoying the shit out of him.

191–200—Holy. Cow. I. Can't. Believe. I've. Actually. Done. 200. Sit-ups!

I am now lying flat on my back again, and I'm filled with many conflicting thoughts and emotions, most of which I'm attributing to a heart that's banging up against my chest in protest, trying to remind me that I'm not the type who exercises—well, at least not regularly. Should I continue? Should I give it up? Should I call a few of my friends and tell them that I just did two hundred sit-ups? Would they even believe me if I told them? Should I get up and go and look at my stomach now? Maybe I should make a pit stop by the mirror on my way to the bedroom, because maybe I should go and take a nap.

I decide to try to do fifty more, so at least I can say that I got to the halfway mark, and, honestly, two hundred fifty sit-ups by a noncelebrity could very well be the *equivalent* of doing five hundred. I mean, after all, I'm pretty sure that one of my sit-ups equals, in terms of weight being lifted up, say, two of Cameron Diaz. (Okay, I'm exaggerating, but honestly, have you seen her jeans? She's got these legs that are as thin as signposts.)

201–210—I decide that doing fifty more was a stupid idea, I should have just lied.

211–220—Weird cramp, am seriously considering stopping.

221–230—I am thinking that if I stop now, I could very easily lie and say I did two hundred fifty. I mean, two hundred thirty rounded up is totally two hundred fifty, and two hundred fifty rounded up is definitely three hundred, and from there, well, you get the picture!

231–240—I am saved by my phone ringing, I try to hurry through these ten so I can answer my phone, as I *was* expecting an important call.

241–250—Did I? Or didn't I? You decide.

It's now around four o'clock in the afternoon and I have just awoken from an hourlong nap. I am disoriented a bit, as I don't usually nap, but it seemed reasonable, as I'm sure celebrities nap a lot—well, in between shopping and getting their nails done. What I do notice, besides my dog, who is apparently pretty peeved that he's late for his afternoon stroll, is that my stomach hurts. I wonder if this is what it feels like when stomach muscles begin to grow. Wow, that was fast. Or perhaps the pain is a mere protest from my belly-fat cells, reminding me that they have rent control and if I think they're just going to bail out over a few sit-ups, then I should think again.

While walking my dog I think about the trappings of the rich and famous. Whereas most women I know have a little voice in their head always commenting on food *(Say no. Don't eat it. You'll regret it. Hell, if you're gonna eat it, then at least get the big piece)*, I'm assuming the little voices that speak to celebrities must use bullhorns *(HA HA, WHY ARE YOU EVEN THINKING ABOUT PASTA? YOU, BABE, ARE NEVER GOING TO EAT PASTA AGAIN. BOOHAHAHAHA!)* and probably aren't all that nice. It's probably these same bullhorns that bully them around about exercise, too. I remember reading an interview with Cher once where she said that she loved chocolate, but she knew that if she ate just a little piece of chocolate she would have to put in an extra five miles on the treadmill. Meaning five miles more than what she *normally* does?! I mean, I have a special relationship with chocolate, but if I had to run five miles for a piece of it, I'd, well, let's just say, I wouldn't. (I can be very practical when it comes to exercise.)

Hmmmm, so perhaps Britney's recent "acting out" was all due to a rebellion—not from her stage mom, her manager, or all of her fans, who once believed she was a "good girl"—but from the five hundred SIT-UPS A DAY. EVERY DAY. That's probably why she even considered getting married without a prenup, because she is smart enough to know that the chance of a celebrity marriage working out is basically ZERO, so in all actuality what she was doing was wanting to lose half of her money since she

probably had some sort of mathematical equation that figured out how many sit-ups you have to do every day based
on the number of millions you have in the bank.

Suddenly, I feel kinda bad for Britney.

Okay, I'm done feeling sorry for Britney.

When I get home I decide that perhaps it isn't so bad being over thirty and not having several hundred million in
the bank, if the alternative means that I wouldn't be able to
have Old El Paso taco night with my husband *(HA-HA.
YOU CAN'T EAT TACO SHELLS. YOU CAN NEVER
EAT TACO SHELLS AGAIN!)*. Or if it means that I had
to do another two hundred sixty sit-ups today. And then five
hundred more tomorrow!

As you can see, I was lying earlier about doing my last
ten to make it two hundred fifty. (Big surprise, huh?) But
now I decide, why not get real and at least sweat through
those last ten, just for the principle of it? And to celebrate
the fact that I will never put myself through this sort of tor-
ture again (well, without getting paid, or being thrown in
prison). So...

241–250—These last ten are for you, Britney. Just remember what Mama must tell you all the time: *We're just
jealous*.

ATTACK OF THE SQUIGGLY WHITE LINES

There is no love connection between me and my knees. None. And on this particular morning, I've noticed that I have these strange white squiggly lines on them. I lick my finger and rub at one, thinking perhaps it's just an issue of dryness, but nothing happens. Five minutes later I am still staring at them when my husband, Cosmas, comes into the bedroom after his morning shower.

"What are you doing?"

I find this question absurd, as my face is now two inches from my knees, and instead of answering I just point to one of the lines.

He does not have his glasses on, and so he bends his wet

head close to where I'm pointing and says, "Ew, what's that?"

I pull my knee violently away, almost clipping him on the chin, and do a full roll so I'm now lying facedown in the pillow.

I can tell he's debating whether he should even get involved, contemplating how fast he can grab a pair of boxers and manage to get the hell out of Dodge, but he's wiser now and he knows that if he doesn't deal with the issue at hand immediately it will come back to haunt him, and in all scary movies when the creature of evil gets ignored it will certainly be pissed, and there will be hell to pay.

He puts on his best doctor-patient voice and says, "Let me see."

Facedown in the pillow it is dark and I'm thinking that it's probably time to change the sheets; I flop back over like a sullen fish. I lie very still as he's inspecting my knees, and I say nothing as he rubs on one of the lines with a wet finger and I'm now debating whether he's using a fallen drop from his wet hair or his own spit.

Suddenly he stiffens, and then pulls back very quickly, as if one of the white lines has leapt off my knee and lunged for his jugular. He's cracked the case, but he doesn't want to tell me.

"It's nothing," he says through clenched teeth as he's frantically searching for boxers and a pair of socks in the top drawer of his dresser.

"Killer knee fungi?" I'm the type who needs to know exactly what I'm dealing with, as I'm more scared of the unknown than anything else.

This time he says it in a quieter, breathy, almost begging please-let-her-drop-it tone. "It's nothing."

I leap out of bed like a giant anaconda in a bad sequel movie, hoping that the surprise element will scare him into submission. I now have him pinned from behind, and the boxers and socks are lying at his feet. He stares at them wistfully.

"Tell me," I whisper, trying to sound as much like a giant anaconda as I can, having only seen bits and pieces of the movie on cable when channel surfing.

"You don't want to know" is his firm reply, and he tries to wiggle his way out of my grasp.

This is my moment of morning truth, this is where I should be wise enough to have faith that my husband, who after four years of marriage knows me and my moods better than anyone else on the planet (not including my best female friends, of course), and I should just do the grown-up thing and take his advice and let the whole thing go. Maybe I'm not the anaconda after all; maybe I'm the victim in this situation. And maybe it's better to be the clueless one—the one who just stands there while a giant anaconda is right behind her sizing up its prey, and all the while she is simply wondering why everyone else is staring at her with huge unblinking eyes and waving their arms about—*What, do I have something on my shirt? Wait, is my hair messed up? Does someone have a mirror?* Nah, I'm so not the clueless type. I'm the one on the couch who is always screaming at the TV at the clueless one. *STUPID GIRL! STOP WORRYING ABOUT YOUR HAIR! THERE IS A GIANT ANA-CONDA RIGHT BEHIND YOU! HOW CAN YOU NOT KNOW? CAN'T YOU FEEL ITS STINKY SNAKY BREATH ON YOU? RUN!*

I let him go, and after a moment he bends down and picks up his boxers and socks and walks out of the bedroom. I sink back in bed and listen as he continues to get ready for work. In my head I am giving myself orders. *REMAIN CALM. BREATHE.* I breathe deeply, telling myself that the hysterical girl in scary movies always dies (monsters don't like whiners, either), and it's the levelheaded, practical, pretty-but-not-too-pretty girl who makes it through the ordeal in one piece. That's me. Practical. Pretty (with makeup and B-movie lighting), but not too pretty. I decide to make a list of every bad thing I know that involves knees.

Cellulite. Cancer. A new type of varicose veins that aren't blue but white. Rash. Sleep lines. Tropical knee disease that involves elephants (elephants do not have good knees). Poisonous bug bite (hmmm, I really should change the sheets).

"Okay, I'm leaving. Have a good day." I hear the door open and he pauses. Yes, there he is standing at the door and wondering whether he's ever going to see me again. Or he's wondering whether he should lie and say he's going to get help, all the while knowing that it's too late. But in actuality, he's standing there because he knows I'm going to ask, and he knows that he's going to have to tell me. I can picture him staring at the stairwell, three quick flights, two doors, and he's outside and free for at least ten hours.

I play it brave. I play it nonchalant. I play it like Sigourney Weaver alone with a bunch of drooling aliens and only one round of bullets left on her bullet-belt thingie. I tell him to just yell it out and then run like hell.

"Stretch marks!" The door slams.

I am momentarily relieved, and in my head I'm thinking, *Oh, they're just stretch marks*. I then move to thinking that I've never actually seen a stretch mark before, and of course I've never even heard of anyone who has stretch marks on their knees. I stare at my dog, Wendell, who is staring back at me from the end of the bed. *Don't worry, I've got your back*. (This is what I'm pretending he's saying, but in actuality the look is more akin to *I'm gonna nap a little more; let me know when it's time to go outside*.)

Saying it out loud always makes something real. I'm not sure why, but it does. Because when you're hanging off the side of the boat staring at your reflection in the murky water and trying to decide whether you might want to start parting your hair on the other side of your head, thinking you might get a little more lift and volume out here in the damp jungle, where bad-hair days were invented, and someone walks up and says, "Hey, don't lean too close because there's a giant anaconda in the water that's eventually going to kill most of us," you can't quite process what they're saying—well, not until you say it out loud. "Hey, do you think that if I part my hair on the left side instead of the right... Did you just say (gulp) 'giant anaconda'?"

Stretch marks.

I freak.

STRETCH MARKS?! STRETCH MARKS!! EW! GROSS! HOW THE HELL DID I GET STRETCH MARKS ON MY KNEES?! HOW DID THIS HAPPEN? WHAT DOES IT MEAN? DO I HAVE FAT KNEES? DID I HAVE FAT KNEES? DID I HAVE FAT KNEES AND NOW I DON'T (which, granted, might not be such a bad thing)*? WAIT, WHEN DID I HAVE FAT KNEES AND NOT KNOW? WAS I KIDNAPPED BY ALIENS WHO INJECTED FAT INTO MY KNEES FOR RE-SEARCH AND THEN THEY SUCKED IT ALL BACK OUT AND THEN RETURNED ME WITH STRETCH MARKS?* (In case you are wondering, I'm not really the type who believes in alien abduction, though of course I have noted that most alien life-forms are portrayed to be quite thin.)

Moments later, I am Googling "stretch marks on knees" and I'm immediately comforted that a page of links shows up. Well, at least I'm not the only one.

What I learn is that stretch marks are actually small breaks in the collagen that is beneath the skin that are caused by, duh, stretching. Obviously, they are most common in the stomach area due to pregnancy, but they also appear when people have growth spurts and gain weight.

Oh.

Interesting.

How funny, I don't feel taller. (Denial is a beautiful thing.)

This is the end of the bad sequel, not because the ordeal is over, but because every bad sequel has to be ended in some ambiguous but hopeful way, leaving room for a Part 3. So this is the point where the heroine is walking out of the jungle, all her friends are dead, but she has survived, and she now genuinely believes she can go back to her normal life. So there she is, walking toward the one lone hut in the distance that has smoke curling out of the chimney (even though it's like a zillion degrees in the jungle, but how else would she know that someone was there, because everyone knows that no one leaves a fire untended), and then fifty feet behind her you see the tall grass moving in a way to suggest…OHMYGOD, THE GIANT ANACONDA THAT HAS LIVED IN THE WATER FOR THE LAST TWO MOVIES HAS NOW EVOLVED INTO A GIANT ANACONDA THAT LIKES DRY LAND AND IT'S FOLLOWING HER THROUGH THE TALL WEEDS! WE NEED ANOTHER MOVIE SO WE CAN FIND OUT WHAT HAPPENS!

I am now stark naked under my comforter with a flashlight, inspecting every square inch of my body for more stretch marks. Of course, this would be easier if I were willing to stand in front of my full-length mirror, which is on the inside door of my kitchen closet, but I'm not. Standing naked in front of full-length mirrors is reserved for teenage girls waiting for their boobs to grow, twenty-somethings with high metabolisms, hypochondriacs who are obsessed with moles, and rail-thin beautiful people who really have to work to grab some skin in between their fingers just so they can sigh dramatically, blow their beautiful blond wispy bangs out of their smoky, wide-set eyes, and say, "Guess who needs to do more ab work?"

The rest of us, the ones whose abs have been unemployed for a long, long time, like to inspect ourselves a little bit at a time. So after a half hour of inventive mirror placement, I have come to the conclusion that I only seem to have stretch marks on my knees. And after much consideration and lots of thoughtful thinking (and a bag of Hot Fries—if a bag of Hot Fries is eaten under the covers and no one sees me, do those calories count?), I have decided that the stretch marks on my knees are the direct result of the fact that I have a rather unladylike tendency of sitting in my desk chair with one of my knees up by my chin and the other tucked Native American style underneath me, and granted, such an uncouth sitting style probably wouldn't snap my knee collagen on its own, but I'm sure it had help from my jeans, which probably at times have been a little too tight (and perhaps my normal knee fat has contributed a smidge, too). Ta-da. Mystery solved. Not exactly a happy ending of me sashaying about in a short little skirt, but then again, I'm over thirty. I don't wear short little skirts, and I certainly don't sashay.

Cue scary music.

So in the movie version of *Attack of the Squiggly White Lines, Part 3,* there could never be such a dull and highly rationalized ending, so taking a bit of Hollywood artistic license (isn't it funny that they still use the word "artistic"?), we'll have the giant anaconda be a fan of Hot Fries as well.

Enough said. (The happy ending in this version is that while everyone knows that calories consumed while under a blanket really do count, what is good to know for future reference is that they certainly don't count if you are promptly eaten by a giant anaconda.)

YOU GO TO YOGA

You tried yoga once before, but it was years ago—before it became so popular with the celebs—and you hated it. You had positioned yourself along the far-left wall of the exercise room (close to the door for easy escape) and you weren't just tight with the stressors of everyday life, no, you were also tight with skepticism. After the teacher made the announcement that she welcomed all moaning, and that in fact she expected it, you knew that you were totally out of your element. Like you were really ever going to moan in a room full of strangers (in fact, the only time you ever remember moaning among people you didn't know was while staring through the glass at all the different types of cheesecake at The Cheesecake Factory, and you knew then that no one had heard you because everyone else was doing it too). You made it through the Om opening and the first ten minutes, but when the guy next to you moaned like, well, never mind that, let's just say it was loud, you grabbed your right calf and pretended to have a cramp. Of course, you fake-limped on the wrong leg out the door, but you didn't care. You just gave a little sayonara wave to the teacher to say good-bye and good riddance.

But seven years have passed and you're more open-minded now, since you hate running on the treadmill. In fact, let's face it—you hate running of any kind. Just to sweeten the deal, one of the best yoga studios in the country happens to be ten minutes away from you and you've been noticing all the people walking around the neighborhood with towels around their necks, looking beatifically thin. For a long time you figured there must be a swimming pool nearby (yes, they were actually that wet), and finally you ran into a neighbor who gave you a five-minute testimonial on how yoga changed her life by thinning out her thighs.

Never one to scoff at the promise of thin thighs, you decide to give yoga another try. So after a few phone calls and a bit of Internet surfing you decide to check out the Baptiste Power Yoga Institute, and you show up for one of the introductory classes. The waiting room is filled with yoga types, men and women who probably don't eat meat or, by the looks of them, much of anything else. They look lean and hungry, and you decide that even though you have a weight advantage on them, they could probably kick your ass if you met up with them in a dark alley. There is incense burning (of course), and you sit on a bench and take off your shoes and socks and place them in one of the cubbyholes next to one of the many pairs of tan suede Birkenstocks (yoga people really like Birkenstocks).

You pay for the class, rent a mat, and buy a bottle of water. You ask the beautiful woman who is all long legs and skinny arms who is obviously the gatekeeper, as she is perched on a stool by the door and seems to be in charge of taking the poker chips that you have to give over for entry (honestly, I wouldn't think yoga types would ever sneak in without paying first, surely crime karma is bad, no?). Bashful like a fat new kid on your first day of school, you ask the gatekeeper where you should sit, and she gives you a Zen smile and says anywhere is fine—then wags a bony finger in your face—but not the first row. The first row is for the advanced people. You think about getting offended over the fact that she naturally just assumed you couldn't possibly be advanced, but you decide to let it go because you're pretty sure it's obvious.

When you enter the room you are assaulted by a wave of moist hot air and you begin to sweat almost immediately, which you're not thrilled with, as you're not a big fan of sweat in general. The room is almost full already and you look around and realize that you probably have little in common with anyone in this room, and you give yourself a stern lecture about trying to keep an open mind. Being negative is a defense mechanism that kicks into gear when you don't have anyone to make bad jokes to, and you think to yourself that if you can just survive the class you'll have plenty of new material to entertain your nonyoga friends with. You may not be very athletic, but you are very good at making fun of those who are.

You find a space by the far back wall and you roll out the mat that you rented for a dollar. It looks like it's basically been to hell and back, and you try not to think about the hundreds of other people who have sweated on your mat before you. Most people are already in some position on their mat—some in downward dog, others lying on their backs with their feet together and their knees splayed out; there are even a few people who are balancing on their heads.

Suddenly, you are filled with the intense desire to leave, but it's too late because the teacher has just walked into the room. Her body mesmerizes you; she's just so skinny, but not skinny in that sickly I-could-snap-you-in-half way, but skinny in that way where you know she'd make sweatpants look hot. By the time you get to her face, which is attractive (and in her thirties—rock on, girlfriend, you've got the body of a twenty-year-old), you even have to admit that she seems pretty serene. Yes, this is what a teacher should be— a walking billboard that says do what I do, and you too will look great in jeans. You stay.

Pleased that there are no mirrors on the wall so you can't see yourself in relation to everyone else, you take a deep breath and decide to just go along for the ride. The woman next to you gives you a smile, which you first take as a good sign, but then wonder whether in her head she's smiling because she knows you're an impostor who will soon be sorry that she ever walked barefoot into this sacred place where the skinny plant-eaters come to pray.

The teacher's voice is husky in a way that might imply that she smokes, but you doubt it. Starting out in the basic position of downward dog, you try to concentrate on what the teacher is saying as opposed to staring at your unpolished toes. She says that you should free your mind from the outside world. She says that you should find your third eye and focus inward. (Though she does not tell us where we are supposed to find this third eye, and you try to get rid of the picture in your head of some extra eye that is placed haphazardly on your brain somewhere.) She says that we should feel proud that we have made the time to practice yoga today and that ninety percent of the battle is just showing up. (This is when you think that if what she said is true you could actually just pick up and leave, but you're sort of scared of the teacher, so you don't.)

You start to focus on the fact that you are already drenched in perspiration and the class has barely begun, and you wonder whether sweat is running up everyone else's nose the same way it is running up your own. As each position is held for minutes at a time, you now have a little bit of time to check out the people around you. The woman in front of you has on a whole matching yoga outfit—black pants, tiny orange top to show off her arms, even a matching orange headband. You lose yourself in the notion that if you stick with yoga for a while you might one day get to shop for cute little matching yoga outfits too, and this gives you your first real moment of peace.

In the standing positions you find that your thighs are literally shaking with strain, and you wonder whether the people around you would help you once all your toes snap off your foot and go rolling about the floor. You find yourself teetering and swaying a lot and you have visions of a yoga domino effect that will happen once you go crashing to your left and into the sinewy girl next to you who doesn't have the matching outfit, but does have a little flame tattooed on her ankle. One thing to note about yoga people is that they seem to have a lot more tattoos than the general population, and their tattoos are not sexy and playful (no little roses on their hipbones or butterflies on the napes of their necks); no, most yoga people either have the little flame symbol on their ankle or at the base of their spine, peeking out of their little flame-logo yoga pants, or else they have some Chinese characters printed on the backs of their shoulders.

You wish you could read Chinese, as you now want to know what kind of messages people stamp on their bodies. Are they one-word yoga slogans like Peace, Serenity, Patience? Or are they bolder testaments like Look How Tight My Ass Is, Limber Girls Do It Better, or maybe even something like I Started Yoga to Meet Hot Indian Guys but Now It's Changed My Life? You wonder how the people who get these Chinese proverbs inked onto their bodies even get proof that they actually say what they paid for them to say. Maybe it's a scam and they are basically walking advertisements for local Chinese businesses.

You now have sweat running into your eyes; either that or you are crying from sheer exhaustion. You fake a little twist so you can take a peek at the clock on your far left and you notice that the hour is almost up, and surely the class will soon be over. You start to feel elated that you have survived the class and have probably managed to lose at least two pounds of water. Maybe that's why yoga people always look so thin—they are all dehydrated from having every ounce of excess water squeezed and stretched out of their bodies.

The teacher says that it's now time for the floor-exercise portion of the class and everyone gratefully drops to their mat, and you are relieved that you aren't the only one who was about to collapse. You gulp at your water and give another quick glance at the clock and notice that the class is now running five minutes over. Well, it makes sense that yoga people aren't superstrict about time, leaving that to the rest of us who are uptight and always on a schedule (how else would we know when it's time to eat?). The woman with the flame tattoo on her ankle who smiled at you earlier seems to be mouthing something at you. What is she saying? You try to blink the sweat out of your eyes so you can focus on her bobblehead (she's so skinny her head does look a little large, and she's got a mouth that would impress Julia Roberts herself). Is she telling you that it's unwise to wear blue underwear under light gray tights when you sweat a lot? Is she telling you that she was once a little flabby like you, but look at her now (man, these yoga girls really like attention)? No, Miss Eternal Flame Tattoo Girl is telling you that yoga class is ninety minutes, not sixty, and so we have a ways to go.

She registers the look of dismay on your face and does her best to look sympathetic as she arches her back to become a human Cheerio. You are not attempting this particular exercise, as you think that the ability to walk upright after class might come in handy. So instead you're lying on your stomach pressed up against a smelly mat and trying not to cry. There is no possible way in hell that you are going to be able to continue to contort your body around for another twenty-five minutes. And surely you have already depleted all your sweat reserves, and you shudder to think about how embarrassing it is going to be when the paramedics arrive to try to peel you off the floor.

This is the point when one of the teacher's assistants shows up by your side and puts her sweaty hand on your shoulder and asks whether you are okay. You tell her you're not sure and that this is your first class and you now totally understand why they make you sign a waiver ahead of time. She gives you a you-poor-chubby-baby smile and says that you are doing fine and that everyone has to be a beginner sometime. Good God, is this how all yoga people talk? Maybe there is a handbook on how to speak fortune cookie. You try to give her a smile, but you find that you are too tired to do so, and you think that if you were to get a tattoo one day perhaps you would ask to have those very words put on your shoulder, or maybe you could have the words I Don't Brake for Skinny Girls instead. Oh, forget the tattoo; maybe it's time to start thinking about the phrasing for your tombstone.

The teacher's assistant has left and come back, and she is

holding your bottle of water, which she has just refilled for you. She gives you another sweaty shoulder rub and says that it is important to stay hydrated since the room is heated to over ninety-five degrees. You take the water thankfully and begin to guzzle it down, and in doing so you start to feel a little bit better. The rest of the class is doing abs now, and you roll over onto your back and try your best to join in. No way that a bunch of yoga people are going to get the better of you (especially now that you've had fifteen minutes to rest and the class is about to end). And you try your best to block out the fire in your belly by reciting "Ninety-nine Bottles of Beer" in your head to help pass the time.

Finally, mercifully, you have reached the end of class. The last five minutes are spent lying on your back with your eyes closed and trying to "come back into your own body," which you find interesting because you wonder if you came back again whether it might be possible to "come back" into someone else's body—like maybe the girl two rows in front of you who can actually pull off turquoise tights and a red top. The one with the, you guessed it, Chinese characters tattooed on her right shoulder that probably say, You'll Need All Three Eyes to Appreciate My Abs. You can't help but smirk at your own superficiality, but you don't care if the yoga people notice; you doubt you'll ever see them again.

HAIR TODAY,
HAIR TOMORROW

I'm not the type of woman who's really into my hair. I mean sure, I'm happy to have it, and yes, I'd hate to lose it, but in general I'm not that obsessed with it. Since I am of Asian descent, my hair is very straight and very dark (though I don't have that super-inky jet-black hair like some Asians do). When I was little I had long hair and bangs (in the '70s and '80s bangs were very in) and I normally wore it in ponytails—usually one, but sometimes two (okay, side ponytails were never very in, but I was young, what did I know?). As a teenager I remember mooning away and wishing that my hair were wavy like Jaclyn Smith's and Farrah Fawcett's, and I tried to feather it, but it took a lot of hair spray and the results were more shellacked than feathery. I did convince my mom to let me perm my hair once, and even though she told me I would regret it, I didn't believe her and I begged the way you do when you're fourteen and you think that having curly hair will change your life. The perm did change my life; I looked like a Korean poodle with glasses (which wasn't exactly the look I was going for).

In my twenties I put the bangs to rest and pretty much had the standard New York Korean-girl hair, which was long and straight. I got a lot of mileage in nightclubs flipping my hair from side to side and doing the minimalist Asian-girl dance where I was barely moving (sweating was a no-no), and I kept my very red lips in a continual pout. I was a dime a dozen, surely.

The best thing about my hair was that I had very minimal upkeep; in fact, I rarely went to the salon, as I usually asked a friend to trim an inch off the ends from time to time, but that was about it. I didn't blow it dry because it took too long. I didn't buy expensive shampoos and conditioners because it didn't seem necessary. My hair was always the same.

My best friend, Laura, who was certifiably hair obsessed, told me on several occasions that she envied my no-nonsense approach, but once she did ask if I was ever bored with it. I remember finding her question odd at first, mainly because I had never really given it much thought, but then I decided that perhaps I shouldn't be so laissez-faire about it. Hair, after all, was normally a pretty big deal for a girl.

For the next few weeks I closely observed Laura's hair routine, which was far more complicated and time consuming than I had ever imagined. She had a special shampoo and conditioner; she had a special volumizing spray that she used while her hair was wet; and every day she did the same thing: shampoo, condition, towel-dry, apply volumizing spray, then blow-dry. Sometimes she added a fine mist of hair spray, but usually not, because she said too much product limited the natural swing. She did not blow it dry the way I sometimes did when it was freezing outside and I was late for class (I was always late for class), which was that I hung my head upside down and just blasted the heat. No, how Laura blew-dry her hair was far more choreographed than that. She used a special brush, and as she blew she pulled her hair this way and that. She looked like a maestro conducting a symphony, and once I even played Beethoven while I watched, but the joke was lost on her. Or maybe it wasn't; she was all business when it came to her hair.

I will say that her silky blond hair always looked great, but I will also say that someone like me (and most males on the planet) would have no idea what she went through for her hair. After a few days it was my turn to ask her a question, which was whether her hair was really worth the effort. She did not hesitate, not for a second; her answer was "absolutely."

My hair lessons continued as I came to find out that she was not a natural blonde; well, let me rephrase, she was once a natural blonde, but in her twenties it was getting darker and so she did what the majority of blonds on the planet do—she started to get highlights. Highlights are very costly and they are a very big deal—getting the right color, getting them put on just so—all for the sake of making sure that her hair looked very natural. I guess it worked, because for years I had no idea.

What I learned about my hair after learning so much about her hair was that maybe my hair was a little boring. So I began to experiment—I learned to hot-roll it, sponge-curl it, and even to tie it up in rags so it would look all kinky and windblown. But the curls never lasted, so I eventually grew bolder and finally I cut it. First I went short. HUGE MISTAKE. Forget Korean poodle, think Korean butch chipmunk. I grew it back out long, and kept it that way for a while (until I got over my chipmunk trauma), and later joined the rest of the nation and got the Rachel, which was better, but required me to actually learn how to blow-dry my hair. But eventually I grew irritated by the upkeep, and usually let it all grow back out again—long, straight, and boring.

In the first year of my thirties I experienced a small identity crisis, which was that I gained a little weight and, since clothes shopping became more depressing and less fun, I began to look for new ways to keep myself looking current. I will admit that even though I said I had no problem with turning thirty, I did feel a little wistful at times that I didn't really do anything totally wild and irresponsible, which when you're twenty-something you can do without much consequence *(She's just sowing her oats)*. But when contemplating doing something a little off the beaten path (we're still talking about hair here, it's not like I was toying with being a swinger or anything) in your thirties, you always risked having other women think that you were in denial over your age and just desperate to still be young by trying to look young.

I once worked at a small marketing company and one of the older women that I worked with (she was in her late forties or early fifties, it was hard to tell) still had long blond hair and wore lots of sassy colorful pantsuits. And to her face all her peers would say, "Oh, Ellie, I love that big bold chunky fuchsia necklace. You're just too stylish for words." But what they said behind her back (take note, people, assistants may not make much money, but we certainly can hear) was, "She looks ridiculous. I mean, that hair and those outfits, how old does she think she is? Honestly, no respectable woman past the age of thirty still wears her hair like that." I remember feeling sorry for Ellie a little, not because she didn't dress age appropriately (that I applauded), but more because her friends were obviously not really her friends.

Ellie popped into my head soon after my thirtieth birthday when I went to the hair salon (yes, I now paid to have it cut) and I decided that maybe it was time to cut my own long hair. Now, since I didn't have the cheekbones to pull off short hair, I decided to just take the middle road and cut about four inches off so that my hair fell an inch below my shoulders. So where I used to have straight long boring hair, I now had straight medium-length boring hair. The dissatisfaction grew.

I began to secretly covet the idea of getting blond streaks in my hair, which I know is so twenty-something trendy club kid, because there ain't nuthin' natural about blond streaks on an Asian girl. But I felt trapped by my desire because I felt that I had passed my window to have them written off as just a youthful whim. (Apparently, you get far fewer whim passes the older you get.)

So I called Laura to ask her opinion. I said, "What do you think about blond streaks in general?" Laura, who is no dummy, knew that I was using best friend code speak and she played along. "Well, they're not that trendy anymore, but I can see how they might be fun for a while." Okay, she was giving me some room to run. "What do you think about blond streaks on the over-thirty crowd, civilian, not a celeb?" (Obviously, celebs had different hair bylaws altogether.) "I think they might look a little young, but hey, it's your hair. You should get them if you want them." Oops. She had broken out of code speak and outed me.

It's silly that I was embarrassed, but I was. I mean, surely I had more important things to think about than whether or not I should get blond streaks put into my hair. I thought about it for a moment.

"I think I'm going to do it." And I believe her response was, "You go, girl. Send pictures." But I didn't do it. And two years passed and suddenly, again, I felt the urge and this time I didn't even call in to ask permission, I just booked an appointment at the salon.

I love going to the hair salon these days, not because I'm so into my hair now (well, I am a bit more, but I'm far from obsessed), but more for the experience. It's just nice to get out of the house and into the bustle of beauty. My salon has all the new magazines (even the trashy ones like *Star*), they offer you cappuccino, they have a patio where you can go and smoke out in your robe. But best of all, I've started a relationship with a hairstylist. Her name is Janna. She was twenty-one when I met her and at first I felt so old (and a little freaked out; I mean how long had she been cutting hair on real people—Barbie didn't count), but soon I found her to be completely entertaining. I liked hearing her talk. She told me about her twin sister's eating disorder. She told me about the new boots she found on sale. She told me that her mom still wanted to give her a curfew. She told me about her nights out at clubs. She told me she was saving up her pennies for a boob job. She told me she wanted to move to South Beach. We bonded over our love of celebrity gossip and TV shows like *The OC* and *Sex and the City*.

So when I went in and asked for blond streaks, I was surprised to see her hesitate. Oh no, please tell me I wasn't going to get the how-old-are-you question. Luckily, she wasn't obtuse enough to ask that, but what she did ask was whether I understood that bleaching out chunks of my hair wasn't the greatest thing to do in the world, this coming from a girl who never had the same hair color whenever I visited. She then informed me that there was no way that blond streaks were going to look natural in my hair. Okay, maybe I was going through some sort of mini emotional breakdown, but that didn't mean I was suddenly an imbecile.

I reassured her that I knew that it wasn't going to look natural, and that in fact I was sick of natural, and maybe fake artifice was what I needed. She excused herself and went to go talk to one of the senior colorists, and I watched as they stood huddled in the back, talking about me. She appeared again by my side and said that she and the colorist had spoken and they were of the shared opinion that perhaps I might want to rethink the blond and instead go for some nice caramel streaks, which would look much more "natural." I explained that any Asian woman who had any hair color other than dark brown/black (or gray) could never, would never, pass as natural.

And on the spot, I decided to put in red streaks instead—not the subtle red, but the fake rock-star red—which I hoped I could get away with since I was going to only put in a few streaks, as opposed to the all-over dye job that metal-band groupies sport.

And so it was done. After two and a half hours I walked out onto the street the proud owner of six shocking-red streaks in my hair. (Some were hidden under the top layer of my head so they could peek out when I did sexy up-dos.) I felt pretty good, not great, and certainly not like a rock star, but I was happy that I acted on a whim and no one was pointing and laughing at me on the street. And maybe I did get a funny look or two at Starbucks, but whenever I felt someone else's judgment gamma rays heading my way, I thought of Ellie, which always made me smile.

Did it change my life? Not really (but man, that red shampoo really makes you feel like you're the girl in *Psycho* every time you shower—the way it pools by the drain. Ick). I kept them in for about a month, and I finally took them out because it was summertime and the sun and pool chlorine kept changing the red to an ugly orange. I happened to be at my in-laws' beach house when I bought a dark rinse to cover up the streaks. I emerged from the outdoor shower with inky jet-black hair (hey, I knew I could pull that off) and asked my thirteen-year-old nephew what he thought. Better? He nodded. He said he liked the dark better anyway. He said it reminded him of Ashlee Simpson. I smiled and took it as a compliment. At least I was young enough to know who she was.

HOW TO START A NEW DIET, YET AGAIN

Your dieting track has been less than desirable. You've had some successes, but you've had even more failures. And frankly you're sick to death of diets in general. You can't even remember the last pure food experience you've had—meaning that every single food item is always categorized (high protein, high fat, high calories, etc.) and then recategorized (this doesn't work for the induction phase in Atkins, but it works for Phase 1 of South Beach, and I'm pretty sure that it's nowhere near the Zone...), and as soon as you eat it you're already trying to figure out whether you should be super-guilty, a little guilty, or maybe even proud of yourself.

Your brain, which has always struggled with math, has

now been completely taxed by the whole new language of dieting. (Net carbs equals real carbs minus fiber minus sugar alcohol minus ahhhh, who gives a damn.) Your whole experience with the Weight Watchers point system was a complete disaster, since you would always run through your entire point allotment for the day by noon, and then for the rest of the day you would make these slippery little promises to yourself, swearing that you'd make it up tomorrow. (Basically, the lesson from that experience was that you should steer clear of Vegas.)

Lately, you've even been thinking that you might forgo your allegiance to any one diet in particular (you were so good to them, but they were never as good to you) and even try just eating sensibly for a while, though who knows if you even understand what that means anymore. (You may have lost all credibility by carrying around those paper cutouts of chicken breasts from your book on portion-control eating, which you dutifully pulled out every time you ate out, to compare the sizes.)

But you really are tired of the high-speed dieting train that you've been on for the last fifteen years, and you long to just stand on solid ground once more. No more superstitions to follow (you always preferred to start diets on Mondays, and better yet if it was the beginning of the month *and* a Monday—that just gave you chills). No more journals with inspirational quotes from strong women ("A woman needs a diet like a fish needs a bicycle") that you would only use for a week and then toss aside. No more dieting calendars with days crossed off, or smiley faces, and never again will you write, "You Go, Girl!" Why? Because you've gone, gone, gone (all right—but to the fridge, to McDonald's... just never to the freakin' gym).

You feel liberated, and you celebrate with your first Snickers in over three months. You know this because the day before you started your last diet you wrote on your calendar, "My last Snickers bar *ever*." Throw that calendar away. Feel better. Think about throwing away your stack of diet books, but don't because they were expensive. Hide them. Feel better. Put your scale in the closet, and slam the door. You are free.

This newfound feeling of freedom only lasts a few hours, until dinnertime, when you are faced with the challenge of eating without some famous doctor (some famous *rich* doctor) to guide you. Paralyzed, you don't eat anything at all, and instead decide to take a nap, since *not dieting* is very tiring.

You wake up a few hours later to your cell phone ringing, and, as fate would have it, it's one of your friends calling you to tell you she has *great news*. You are always happy when your friends have great news, and you are soon excited about the prospect that she is recently engaged, pregnant, won the lottery, or just bought new shoes. But she tells you that her news is bigger than all those things, and when she says this you know exactly what she's going to say. She's just lost seven pounds on the latest greatest diet, *X*. It takes you only fifteen seconds to cave before you start asking, *begging*, for every single morsel of information. How'd she hear about it? Who recommended it? What is it? Where do you buy the book? When should you start? She is only too happy to share her information, as she is now a dedicated disciple of Diet X, and you grab paper and pen, and tell her that you just so happen to be in the market for a new diet yourself.

Since the bookstores are now closed and you can't buy Diet X until tomorrow, you decide that you should immediately activate your standard ritual—which is what you always do before the start of any new diet. You call this the great ho-ha, which is your own cutesy version of a last hurrah (it used to be called the great Ho Ho, after those Hostess snack cakes, but you once ate a family pack and got really sick so you changed the name a little). Filled with anticipation of being on the way to losing your very own seven pounds, you rush out to the deli so that you can now consume enough junk-food calories to put a bulimic to shame.

You don't go totally overboard, as it's already late and you know that eating right before you go to bed is never wise, so you limit yourself to another Snickers, a bag of Hot Fries, and a pint of ice cream. The guy at the register doesn't bat an eye, because he's owned the store for years now and he's seen much worse than this (he does, after all, live near two universities, and college girls really know how to eat).

Back at home you begin your feast, pacing yourself with the latest issue of *In Style*, and promising that whatever is left by the time you're finished reading the magazine you'll toss. You get through half a bag of Hot Fries and half of the ice cream. You toss them as promised (damn *In Style*'s lack of long-winded editorials), but you throw the Snickers in the freezer just in case of emergency.

Soon you are in bed and you are smiling in the dark. You love the foodfest of the day before a new diet. You love the hope that fills you (or is that the Snickers you just ate in bed?). You love going to the bookstore and buying the shiny new diet book with the little picture of the soon-to-be-rich-and-famous doctor on the back flap, who really does look like a guy who wouldn't steer you wrong. You like going to the section in the store by the registers where you can pick out a brand-new diet journal in which to record your progress. You fall asleep with a smile and chocolate on your face.

The next morning you spring out of bed in total denial of your carb carnage from the night before. You do a little Day 1 diet jig while you brush your teeth. You hum while you put on your jeans, which you know will soon be baggy once you start your diet. You baby-talk to your dog as you feed him breakfast. And then you offer to drive your husband to the bus stop, because you have some time to kill before the bookstore opens at the local mall. Even though your husband is suspicious about your good mood, he has now lived with you long enough (and therefore has lived through many Day 1s of diets) to know that he should not question whatever it is that's making his wife so happy. But on this particular morning, he asks anyway. And when you tell him about Diet X, his face scrunches up like a raisin as he stammers out a protest: "But, but, but," he sputters, "what about yesterday when you called me and told me the great diet crusades were now over, and that I didn't have to be afraid to ask what's for dinner?"

You are in too good a mood to let his doubts deter you, so you call him a silly billy and reassure him that *this* diet will be different. This diet is going to change your life for the better (and hopefully help you knock off ten pounds), and therefore it can only change *his* life for the better, too. He remains skeptical, but lets it go. He knows he is no match for Dr. Diet X, and in the car he is quiet and thoughtful. As he's shutting the passenger-side door, he tells you to have a good day, and reminds you, sweetly, that he loves you just as you are. You smile back and tell him that he will love you even *more* minus ten pounds. Give him a snappy little wave good-bye and wish him a good day!

The rest of the morning is spent reading the new Diet X book from cover to cover. Of course, the first part is a lot of medical jargon that you're gonna skim, as you are not particularly interested in the things actually going on inside your body. No, you're more concerned with the numbers on the scale that you just retrieved from the closet. The afternoon is spent at the grocery store, where you spend a few hundred dollars buying the necessary supplies to get you started on Diet X, and soon it is almost three in the afternoon when you realize, with a breathy little chuckle, that you haven't eaten all day. Now, this really makes you happy, because perhaps just by *owning* Diet X, you are already well on your way to getting rid of all that unwanted fat. And later, after eating a small minimeal that is recommended by

Diet X, you open your brand-new diet journal and begin to write in it.

You write something like this:

Day 1 of Diet X !!!

Today is the first day of my new diet and my goals are to follow Diet X religiously, and in doing so I hope to lose at least ten pounds, though in a perfect world I would really be ecstatic if I could lose fifteen. You then weigh yourself (which is your only depressing moment of Day 1) and you record the number, using an intricate coding system that only you will understand. You do this because you have a fear that you could get hit by a bus one day and you don't want anyone to ever know how much you weigh. Next you take Dr. Diet X's advice and write down everything that you have eaten so far.

Food I Ate Today:

Half a block of tofu (sautéed in a quarter teaspoon of olive oil)

Small salad (oil-and-vinegar dressing)

1 Diet Coke (which is not actually allowed in Diet X, but like you're really going to give up Diet Coke)

7 red seedless grapes

Just looking at this tiny list of food items makes your heart sing for joy, and you wish you could bottle the feeling of Day 1, because you know that then you, too, could get rich. You think about how nice it would be to buy a mansion next to Dr. Diet X and figure that you could wave to each other from your pools.

Exercise is, of course, advised, and you happily go off to the gym, where you walk on the treadmill for fifteen minutes and then you even jog for another ten. You drink a lot of water, because Diet X says that water is a *very* important part of your diet.

By the time you get home, your husband is now home as well, and you find him standing in front of the now bursting fridge, and he does not look happy. Eyeing the contents with more than a little skepticism, he asks what the *plan* is for dinner.

You remind him sweetly that you are starting your new diet today, and that since you are now eating special foods for a while, you won't be able to eat the same thing as him. He takes in this information and then asks you what *he's* supposed to eat. You try not to get annoyed at his persistence and tell him that you just spent hundreds of dollars on food, so you're sure that he can find something. He says he's too tired to cook and says that he's going to order a pizza. This pisses you off because you really don't need a pizza on the premises just now, but you don't want to get into a fight, because Diet X says that stress is bad for your circulatory system, which somehow affects your diet in an adverse way (this is the part you skimmed)....

Later, while you are on the couch recording your events at the gym in your diet journal, you can't help but notice this tiny piece of cheese that is hanging from your husband's beard. Just looking at it makes you realize that you are a little hungry yourself and that it's time for you to go and have some cottage cheese and perhaps another salad. But you don't move. In fact, you are still mesmerized by the cheese string. You think about reaching over and pulling it off, but you don't do it because you are afraid that even the mere contact with this tiny greasy thing will totally set you off and next thing you know you will have knocked back a few slices of pizza, thereby ruining all your progress on Diet X.

You leave the room and retire to your bedroom with your cottage cheese and your lettuce leaves (you don't chop it up and make a salad—because, frankly, you are a little tired by now from the lack of food and the gym visit—and so you just eat it plain, which is truly gross, but somehow you manage). You decide that you should go to bed early, because the sooner you fall asleep, the sooner this day will be over, and the sooner you can wake up to Day 2 of your diet, which is always a little touch-and-go (good because it means you actually survived Day 1, but bad because by now you're probably famished). You go to the bathroom to brush your teeth and wash your face. Your husband is shocked that you are going to bed so early, but he doesn't say anything, as by now he is too stuffed with pizza to even care.

It's now nine o'clock and this is the earliest you've ever gone to bed since the age of ten, but you don't care. You are in bed with your diet journal and your copy of the Diet X book, which you've decided to read again until you fall asleep. Your stomach begins to rumble at ten o'clock and you quiet it down with a large glass of tasteless water. When you went to go get the water your husband was still sitting on the couch, and he gives you a friendly wave. You don't wave back, because he is the enemy now. He is the enemy who has ordered the pizza—the remains of which are now only ten feet away from you.

It's now midnight on Day 1 of your diet, and you can't sleep. You've reread your Diet X book, you've written down a few more thoughts in your diet journal, and you've had two more large glasses of water, which have done little to quiet the rumblings in your stomach, not to mention causing you to make several trips to the bathroom.

At one in the morning you are sitting on the couch in your dark living room. Two feet away from you is a pizza box, which contains two slices of greasy cold pizza. You have no intention of eating them, and yet somehow, you feel better just being near them. You have opened the box a few times and looked at them, and okay, once you even stuck your face into the box and may have even taken a big whiff, but you have not eaten one bite of it. (Okay, you picked off one little mushroom, but mushrooms are totally allowed on Diet X.)

Finally, exhausted from the Herculean effort of not eating the pizza, you fall asleep with the diet journal on your chest. Ta-da! You've officially made it through Day 1 of your new diet! *"You go, girl!"* you've written with a flourish, on a crisp, blank page.

Famous last words...

PANTY LAUGHS

I'm shy. *I lie.* I'm not really. I'm a prude. *I fib.* I'm not totally a prude. How 'bout this: I was raised to believe that sex is a private thing between two people and maybe it's best not to talk about it. (This from a woman who may or may not have had sex on a golf course once. I will confirm nothing.) But seriously, I *do* think that sex is important, and not something to be thought of as dirty or shameful. Which means I'm more than happy to talk about other people's sex lives. Just not my own.

So, I have this friend who's in her thirties, like me. And one day, when reading a magazine (get your mind out of the gutter, she was not reading porn), she learned about this woman (who looked "normal") whose job was to review sex toys. I mean, I guess someone has to review them, right? Anyway, apparently this woman was very matter-of-fact about her job and took it very seriously and rated all sorts of products for looks (ew), how the product worked (double ew), and whether the product specifications were accurate and if it worked the way it was "advertised to work" (Ew. Ew. Ew). You get the picture, right? So, during the article, this Julia Child of sex toys said that one of her favorite products was these remote-control vibrating panties. Yes, that's right. Remote-control vibrating panties.

So, ahem, my friend totally thinks this is a big hoot, and she decides that it would be the perfect gift for her husband on Valentine's Day. She pictures him opening a carefully wrapped box to find the remote control, and she'll be wearing the panties, of course, and then...well, you can only guess. So then she calls up another friend (this is what girls do) to discuss this and her friend confirms that it's hilarious and she thinks about getting one for herself to give to her husband, too. So then they both laugh a lot, which is just a defense mechanism for feeling embarrassed by the whole thing. Not embarrassed because they think sex toys are *shameful* (I mean, they are grown women who are married), but more because they can't hide their own obvious excitement (and I do mean regular excitement, not the sexual kind. Wow, there are lots of double entendres when it comes to sex, huh?)...

So she orders them online, and when she gets the box, she rips it open and discovers that before she takes her new panties on a test drive (it's only natural for her to try them out first before test-driving them in public, right?), she needs to buy two triple-A batteries for the remote control. (You would think that for a hundred bucks they could throw in some freebie batteries.) So she goes out to the store to get the batteries, and when she asks the store clerk for them she gets the very uncomfortable feeling that he knows what she needs them for, and she's mortified. She's also obviously paranoid, because of course the store clerk cannot possibly have any way of knowing what she needs them for (it's doubtful he's a stalker, since he's always chained to that counter). So anyway, she rushes home, puts in the batteries, puts on the panties, and flips the "on" switch.

Obviously, I'm not going to get into the details about my friend's vibrating panties, because I think she might get annoyed at me and that would be bad, because we've been friends a long time and she knows plenty of stuff about me and you never know when she might write a book and get back at me. So anyway, she doesn't actually give her husband his present on Valentine's Day night, because she has a very bad cold and figures that her husband wouldn't be quite as pleased with his new present if there was the likelihood of getting snotted on. So she waits. A few days later she is feeling better and so she dresses up a little and they go out to dinner together at one of their favorite restaurants nearby. She purposely picks a boisterous, crowded place, thinking that the "secret" factor would just amp up the excitement.

So they eat dinner, order dessert, and then she slides her little box across the table. The husband is happy to finally be getting this box, because she's been talking about it an awful lot and he's more than mildly curious about what his wife would find to be the most riotous gift *ever*. So he opens the box, and he looks inside, and he pulls out the tiny black remote control. He gives a small smile and laughs. Then he says thank you. Then he puts it back in the box and pushes it aside, because their desserts have just arrived.

This is *so* not the reaction my, ahem, friend was hoping to get. In fact, she's kinda perplexed. So she leans in and asks her husband what he thinks of her present. He says he's happy with it, and ha ha, he gets the joke. She's still confused, so she leans in again and asks him what he thinks it *is*. He answers very matter-of-factly that he thinks it's a new remote-control thingie for the car. (He had lost his keys a while ago, and has had to open the car manually, and he's complained about it a lot recently.)

Now it's my friend's turn to laugh, too. Ha ha ha. So then she leans in and tells him that the remote control is *not* for the car. Then she raises her eyebrows a few times for emphasis. Now the husband is confused, and he thinks that maybe his wife has been taking too much Theraflu, because she's acting very peculiar. So, gamely, he asks her what the remote control *is* for, if not their car.

She's basically hysterical now with laughter, and she can barely get the words out, and even when she mouths the words "my panties," her husband has no idea what the hell she's saying. The restaurant is very loud. He asks her to repeat it. She does. Still he doesn't understand. Now the husband is getting really frustrated and a little cranky over the whole thing, because he can't help but feel that somehow the joke is on him. (And the à la mode part of his pie is starting to melt.) This is when my friend gets up and scoots in beside her husband and then whispers it into his ear. So now he's finally heard her, but he's still confused. What does that mean, that the remote control is for his wife's panties? So he grabs the box, takes out the remote, flips the switch, and his wife does a little squeal in surprise—you know, basically jumps out of her seat a little. (Hey, you would have too if your panties started to vibrate.)

Now he gets it. But any embarrassment my friend originally felt is *nothing* compared to her husband's embarrassment. He's totally flummoxed, and he points out to his wife that there are kids around at the restaurant—that they are eating in a "family" establishment. He's beyond shocked over the whole thing . . . and he doesn't even feel like having his pie anymore.

Now, no woman wants to hear her husband get a little cranky over vibrating panties, so my friend gets a little huffy, and basically accuses her husband of being a freakin' uptight prig. I mean, it's not like she's table dancing. No one in the restaurant knows she's wearing vibrating panties, for cryin' out loud. Besides, she's pretty sure that ninety-nine percent of the normal husbands of the world would kill to have their wives hand them a remote control for their panties as a present; some may even find it better than pie!

Her husband eventually comes to his senses and manages (via pie) to calm down a little. He explains that he was just a little surprised, because, after all, they weren't two crazy kids living it up in New York anymore, no, they were married now.

This argument does little for my friend; in fact, it makes her even more upset. She then explains to her husband that when they were two crazy kids, they didn't *need* vibrating panties for a laugh. She thinks about throwing a glass of water in his face at this moment, but is sort of afraid that she might inadvertently somehow manage to electrocute herself. (Death by vibrating panties is not the way any woman would want to go.) Instead, she gets up to leave.

The husband soon realizes that he is holding in his hand the best way to stop her in her tracks. He flips the switch. They make up. The rest is, well, none of your business. (Go get your own.) But when she told me the story I found it to be at least as interesting as it was hysterically funny. I mean, why was the whole thing such a big deal? Why was she embarrassed for buying them? Why was her husband such a fool after receiving them? I mean, after all, they were HBO subscribers and loved *Sex and the City* as much as your next garden-variety pervert. Just kidding. They were, after all, two married adults in their thirties, and if anyone needs a little jump (whether by remote or not) it is certainly those who have been married for a while, don'tcha think?

So go crazy. Live it up. Eat, drink, and vibrate, for tomorrow we could all die (and death *before* having vibrating panties would really be a shame, ahem, or so I've been told...).

IF THE BOOT FITS

Awoman's closet is her temple—and mine, lately, has been my Temple of Doom. Okay, I can't lie (well, I *can*, but of course, I'm not going to now)—I am one of those women who sometimes buys clothes a little too snug just so I have some incentive. Which means I'm a woman who has a lot of really nice things that she's never worn and now live in the back of her closet. It's a terrible habit, I know. It's bad for the self-esteem. It's bad for the credit card. And it's a damn shame that I have a kick-ass pair of black suede Manolo Blahnik knee boots that are simply divine and that I have never once worn. Why? Well, y'see (gulp), I can't exactly zip them all the way up. My right calf is particularly chunky.

I'm closer than I was last year, but still I can't quite fit into them.

I feel so lame sharing this dirty little secret, but I have a feeling I'm not alone. I mean, the whole thing happened so fast. I was in New York with my friend Jackie, and we were at the Bergdorf Goodman shoe sale, and it was a total mob scene. Man, if you don't think rich women can get a little trailer-park on each other, then you've never been to one of these sales. So needless to say, there were shoes everywhere, all the salespeople looking beyond grim. Women were grabbing; women were swearing; and a helluva lot of women were trying their damnedest to shove their big old feet into shoes that were just too small. But Jackie and I are regulars at the sale (one year I actually scored five pairs of shoes that were all seventy percent off—although, granted, my bill was still over a thousand bucks), so we knew how to handle ourselves, and more importantly we knew we had each other's back. After more than ten years of friendship and countless hours clocked in stores together, we each knew each other's sizes and tastes. The plan was simple, really—essentially we both just dove in and joined the mayhem, looking not only for shoes that we ourselves loved but didn't need, but also for shoes that the other would love and not need.

I can still remember seeing that left boot in the distance. It was jammed in a corner sitting on top of a pile of discards. I love black suede so much, my breath caught when I saw it. Then, as I drew closer and saw that it was a Manolo boot, my blood pressure skyrocketed. I stopped and took a deep breath, because I knew there was no way in hell that I would be lucky enough to find a pair of black suede Manolo boots *on sale* and *in my size*. (Full disclosure: I wear the most popular size shoe—7.5 or 8, depending on the brand—so it's rare for me to find the really great shoes on sale.) Then I practically dove for it. It was every bit as beautiful up close as it had been from afar, maybe even better. They were totally simple (I don't like flashy boots), had a *stunning* heel and a cut leather trim at the top. Gorgeous.

AND.

THEY WERE IN MY SIZE.

I didn't even look for a chair; I just plopped down on the floor right there, whipped off my left loafer, and shoved my foot in (very Cinderella's stepsister). And it fit! That is, the foot fit perfectly, if just a little bit tight at the top of the zipper. Okay, it was incredibly tight, and I had to do some serious heavy breathing to get it zipped up.

I never look at the price until after I decide whether I like something or not. I don't like it influencing my decision. But the boots were less than a thousand dollars, which seemed pretty damn good for boots of this caliber. And since they were on sale, that meant that the boots were worth twice that (which is not really true, since the markup on shoes is obscene, but whatever). Was I really going to walk my dog around my neighborhood in boots like these? Of course not. But that was entirely beside the point. It was certainly a possibility that something could happen where such boots might be totally necessary one day in my future. In any case, I'm not sure why I was even going through these motions in my head, because I already knew that I was going to buy them. Just as I knew I wasn't going to tell my husband.

Now, I just needed to get my grubby little hands on the other boot. I flagged down a sales assistant and asked for the mate. To keep his eye on the prize I handed over my Bergdorf's charge card to remind him of the commission. And then I waited. As luck would have it, the salesman could not find the mate of my by-now-beloved Manolo boot. As the truth of this set in, I began to pace, like a wild caged animal (albeit a caged animal wearing only one three-inch-high-heeled boot, but you know what I mean). Jackie began to cringe as I refused to accept my card back from the sales associate, telling him that I wanted to buy the boots anyway, and that I was sure the other would turn up by the end of the day, after they'd had a chance to clear up all of this chaos; it was just temporarily lost in the shuffle. But the salesman refused to let me buy just the one boot. And I refused to leave it for some other woman to get. (I wouldn't even consider the very real possibility that somewhere in this room some lady who lunched was wearing my right boot and was looking for the left one, herself.)

Finally, it was decided that he would put it aside for me. Jackie and I would go get lunch and then we'd return to see if the other one had turned up. I only agreed after I extracted the guy's card and his home phone number as insurance. After a quick lunch at the café on the fifth floor, Jackie and I returned, but still no boot. This was the point when I began (with Jackie's help) to scour the place myself, and we left no shoe unturned. An hour passed, and the salesman was about to go on lunch break (which I was sure would consist of a fistful of Xanax), and he suggested that perhaps it was now time for me to give up. He promised that he would certainly call me if it showed up. I didn't want to leave. I didn't leave. Jackie went to go shop and I just sat in one of the chairs and waited it out. Finally, after about a half hour, I decided that it was worth one more search and then I'd admit defeat and would call it quits. I searched through the sale racks. I dug through the piles of discards. I crawled around and looked under chairs. And then, amongst the display of the shoes that weren't on sale, I found it. I almost broke out into song.

Now, after all that effort and wasted time, there was no way that I wasn't taking my boots home, so when I tried on the right boot and I found that I couldn't zip it all the way up, I panicked and quickly pulled down my jeans to hide the ugly fat-calved truth of the situation. I didn't let the salesperson know. I didn't even tell Jackie. I couldn't have told her, because she would have then had to follow the code of shoe-shopping friends and forbidden me to buy them. I bought them anyway, and I was happy. Yes, I was now the proud owner of incredibly expensive gorgeous boots that didn't fit.

Two years have passed since I bought them, and they are still lying in the back of my closet. True, I have lost weight recently, and they are much closer to fitting, but I'm still not quite there. I even hired a personal trainer to try to help get my legs leaner, and when I confessed my dirty little boot secret to her, she was shocked. Shocked that anyone would pay that sort of money for boots. Shocked that anyone could be stupid enough to buy boots that didn't fit. And shocked that I was now spending even more money to try to get into them. I think her exact words were "You're hiring me to help you reduce the size of your calves?" She told me that spot reduction was a myth—just a Moby-Dick in the workout world—and that it was particularly difficult to lose inches in your calves. Was she saying that it was impossible for me to ever fit into my two-year-old boots? She exhaled, staring up into the industrial ceiling lights. No, it wasn't completely impossible, she said, but it wasn't too likely, either.

So that's where I stand now. The left boot fits, the right boot is a smidgeon better, but I still have an inch to go. I've even thought about stretching my boots. Hell, I've thought about wrapping my right calf in Saran wrap to see if I could *sweat off* an inch (I wish I were joking, but I'm actually not). And lately, in my saner moments, I've thought about selling the damn boots on eBay. I mean, thirty-three years old is surely too old to be dealing with dumb shit like this. They are boots, for God's sake, and one can be pretty sure that somewhere out there another woman would gladly pay top dollar for them. So I could get my thousand dollars back. And maybe after that I could buy back some of my pride.

THE PATRON SAINT
OF DIETERS

Librarians have one, epileptics have two, and there is even one for those who misplace their keys. In fact, it is amazing how many ailments (from cancer to cramps), places (from California to Zacatecas, Mexico), and just plain random groups (bridge builders and foundlings) have one, too. But there is no patron saint for those who *really* need one, which is people who are on a diet. Yes, what we need is a patron saint of dieters, or perhaps more accurately, failed dieters. Now, don't think I'm criticizing the Church on this matter (I'm not stupid, nor do I need a lightning bolt with my name on it), but I would just like to say for the record that I think a patron saint should be named for all of us "full-figured" sinners, and though I'm not super-religious, I would be happy to serve on a voluntary basis until one can be named. Or, even better, I could act as the campaign manager for one of my best friends, Jenner (who is Catholic, which I'm sure would help), as she and I have been best-failed-diet-friends since college.

I guess dieters could use Saint Jude (who is the patron saint of desperate situations/lost causes) as well, but wouldn't a woman be more appropriate, given that most dieters are women? I mean, it's really difficult to talk to men about these issues. Whenever I really try to talk to my husband about my weight (though I never give a number) or some new diet I am attempting, he always gets very impatient with me and is quick to say, "You look fine." Which only goes to show that he *totally* doesn't get me, because it's not like I care what *he* thinks about how I look—well, I do, but not as much as I care about how *I* think I look, which is, of course, never thin enough. Anyway, I'm sure Saint Jude has more than enough on his plate for the moment, and doesn't need to hear a lot of bitching and moaning about the evils of control-top panty hose and why low-fat foods never taste all that great.

See, weight is a very personal thing, and everyone's body responds differently to different diets, and everyone has her own set of psychological obstacles that get in the way every time she tries to shed a few pounds. So what we need is a patron saint we can reach out to in all those times of need. A perfect example is when we are at work and some Skinny Bitch colleague comes prancing in with an entire box of Krispy Kremes (Don't you hate the saboteur types?

And of course she herself won't eat a doughnut; in fact, when she says that she had one on the way in, she's lying; she probably gave it to her cabdriver or maybe just threw it away—which should be a mortal sin, because thou shalt not throw away anything with glaze). So, when we go into the break room only to be confronted by that box of yummy fried and frosted dough, we could say a quick prayer to Saint Jenner. "Please, Saint Jenner, help me get to the fridge for more skim milk to put in my second cup of coffee, without reaching for a doughnut as I pass by the box. Please, I really do not need a doughnut, in fact I need a doughnut like I need a piano to fall on me." Hell, perhaps you should pray to her that she does drop a piano on you that will surely break your arms so you physically *can't* grab for one (which is about the only thing that could keep me away from a chocolate glazed Krispy Kreme that has a whipped-cream center)....

If the pope were considering canonizing a patron saint of the Internet (especially with all the porn and spam), then surely he can consider a cause that really plagues so many people. I mean, over twenty million people have bought the Atkins and South Beach diet books alone! "Please, Saint Jenner, help me to stay steadfast and resist the call of the carbs. I swear I can hear an evil army of bagels and bialys calling my name."

And though Saint Jenner might have to spend an awfully disproportionate amount of her time dealing with New York and L.A., she would also be available to all those people in the Midwest who are faced with such bitter winters that there's little choice but to remain indoors with a fridge full of food. "Saint Jenner, I beg you, help me turn my back on the strawberry frosted Pop-Tarts with sprinkles."

I would even help design a fabulous bling-bling medallion that all dieters can wear—maybe a doughnut portrayed with horns and pitchfork, or perhaps just a silhouette of Saint Jenner (looking very svelte) holding her hand out as if to say, *STOP—In the name of your ever-expanding* ass *don't eat that ice cream.* I'm sure it'd be all the rage with celebrities, as they are basically paid to diet.

I suppose what's standing in our way of getting my friend Jenner elected to sainthood is the fact that she's not yet dead (though honestly, in this media-saturated world, perhaps it's not a bad idea to start campaigning early), and the fact that we'd have to demonstrate that there have already been two "miracles" that have happened in her name. I'm assuming that the fact that Jenner and I have demolished numerous cartons of Chinese food and large pizzas in our day probably doesn't count as a miracle (impressive as it is that we never seem to have leftovers). But here are a few "miracles" that might work:

Jenner saw her hunky Crunch-fitness personal trainer for over fifty sessions and never once had an affair. (Though they did go out to dinner, and maybe even held hands, which is not the same.) Even more astounding, Jenner, at the age of thirty-two—after years of complaining about her weight, thighs, and love of carbs—managed the miracle of miracles, which is she actually dropped those LAST TEN POUNDS and got down to her fantasy dream weight! I can bear witness to this miracle, as I was there, admiring how great she looked in pants and the fact that she had absolutely no underarm jiggling whatsoever. I can't tell you how inspiring her miracle weight loss was to me, since I actually knew her and was privy to both the before and the after Jenner. It's a known fact that our metabolisms start to plummet each year after thirty, yet she was able to buck the odds in her thirties and resculpt an ass worthy of the tightest pigskin suede pants. The fact that she may or may not have gained some of it back (and honestly, another woman's weight is definitely no one's business but her own) only goes to prove that she's human and, thus, very empathetic to the cause. What needs to be focused on is the fact that she was able to do it at all in the first place, and if losing fifteen pounds when working full-time and living in NYC (the capital of good eating) ain't a miracle, then I don't know what is.

Furthermore, Jenner, like myself, has probably tried every single fad diet ever created. Fasting? Done it. Low carbs? Of course. That infomercial Hollywood juice-drink diet? Duh. Grapefruit diet? She had the little citrus tongue sores to *prove* it. Calorie counting? You bet, and she can recite the back-of-the-box breakdown on an impressive array of snack foods. Zone, Sugar Busters, Protein Power, etc. If a diet book has been written, she's tried it. And the two of us have spent countless hours on the phone dissecting our current diets of the moment, as well as speculating about the dieting progress of our friends and neighbors.

Which leads me to the main reason why my friend Jenner

should be sainted for her efforts: Anyone can look at failing diets as something to be frustrated by, or even ashamed of, but not Jenner (and not me). No, if anything, she inspires hope that, armed with enough neuroses and faith, she believes that she can both lose the weight and keep it off. (Plus she knows when you need the pep talk versus the tough love. And she knows how to do the latter; one look at her disdainful expression as you pick up a piece of bread would make anyone think twice about eating it. Frankly, I've always waited until she goes to the bathroom before eating my carbs, so strong is her gaze.) I mean, that's what we all need from a patron saint, right? Someone who can offer encouragement for those who need it, as well as steely strength when that's what's required.

So the next time you're stuck in an airport, pushing your brown plastic tray in front of the steaming buffet line at Sbarro, and you find yourself eyeing the spaghetti and meatballs like a teenage girl at the mall armed with her mom's credit card, you can just think of Saint Jenner in her sassy stance, one hand on her bony hip and the other hand held out to say—*Stop. Back away from that tray and go find yourself a salad*. Or, perhaps, should you think about her only after you have demolished every last bit of your spaghetti and meatballs (with, say, a pepperoni pizza slice for appetizer) and are now in the dazed state of carb confusion where you are too full to move (which is good, because there's an ice-cream stand nearby, too)—well, that's okay, too, because she's *been* there herself. And so, like any good saint, she'll never judge you, she'll just act the way any good friend should when you confess your caloric crimes; she'll say, "Babe, it's okay, we've all done the oh-God-why-did-I-just-eat-that thing. Even us saints. And don't you worry now, I'll help you get on a new diet tomorrow. There's plenty of time to suffer yet...."

LET THEM EAT PIE

Sometimes being cute and funny is a good thing, and sometimes it's not. I have a little jokey thing I say about marriage, which is "Life is short, but marriage is long." It's a harmless little statement; a bit glib, I admit, but I don't really mean anything by it—well, except that sometimes I find marriage to be incredibly tedious and I secretly often wonder what the point of it is. I mean sure, it's a nice concept, marrying Mr. Right and living happily ever after, but sometimes when I'm feeling selfish and petty and cranky and mean (which, I guess, is to say, *often*) I think marriage is, I don't know—kinda stupid.

You know how you hear that phrase about marriage being hard work blah blah... Frankly, you hear it so much that you learn to dismiss it reflexively as some moronic cliché that has nothing to do with you and your marriage; it must be intended for all the other yoyos who take the plunge. Then one day you're in your *own* marriage, and you realize that it's not as easy as pie, that it is, in fact, *hard*—and not hard like algebra, but hard like AP Physics (which I didn't even take, it was so hard). And then you begin to feel just a little bit stupid, which is really just the worst thing for someone who thinks they're actually a pretty bright and intuitive person in general to feel. . . .

So then this smart person who now feels stupid (keep up, I'm talking about myself) then proceeds to do something that doesn't just make them feel stupid, but is actually certifiably stupid—and not stupid silly like the Three Stooges, but more stupid like idiotic—like, say, perhaps typing the words "Marriage is stupid" on a little antique manual typewriter you begin playing with in a local antiques store. Now, granted, this is a free country (thank God), and as a citizen you can write practically anything you like without getting arrested. So the fact that I typed those exact words is not in itself the stupid part (more like the mean part, I guess); no, the stupid part is that I happened to type this with my husband only a few feet away.

Now, my husband, who is not stupid (well, occasionally he is, but not right at the moment in question), walks over and admires the typewriter, which isn't too much of a stretch since he knows that I like old manual typewriters, and in fact am the owner of such a typewriter, because he bought one for me at the antiques flea market on Twenty-sixth Street and Sixth Avenue in New York City about ten years ago when we were first starting to date.

This is the point when he starts to lean in for a closer look, which is totally reasonable, and I sort of panic and give him a little shove—no, "shove" may be too strong a word for what I did, let's call it more like a little "push"—at which point he gives me a look of surprise. Anyway, so it's natural that anyone who has just received a little push for no apparent reason would probably soon ascertain that there is in fact a very real reason, and would now want to know what is going on. So he leans in again to get a better look, and this time he solidly plants his feet in a way that can withstand another push (again, it really was a *little* push) from his wife. Aside from picking up the typewriter and making a break for it, I realize there is nothing more that I can do (and haven't I already done enough anyway?), so I just step to the side.

But before I get to the finale of fireworks, let's back up a minute and find out why exactly I had typed my mean little words in the first place. Because any wife who types "Marriage is stupid" for no good reason at all probably deserves what she gets, but going back to the whole "God bless America" thing, perhaps we should say that I'm innocent until proven otherwise. (Obviously, not innocent of typing the actual words, because that I'll admit to, but more that I'm innocent of doing it without a damn good reason.)

I do not have a damn good reason for doing what I did, but I do have a pretty understandable reason (I'm confident that a jury of married women would let me walk). Right before we entered the antiques store (which, by the way, I didn't even want to go to in the first place because I'm not a huge fan of antiques stores but am always forced to go to them all the time with my husband, who loves them), we were eating lunch at a local diner. And though we were not fighting, we were not having a particularly fun time either. In fact, we were doing that dreadful thing that married couples sometimes do, which is we were just eating and not talking. At all.

C'mon, you know exactly what couples I'm talking about, because whenever you're out to dinner at a crowded restaurant there is always at least one. These couples are particularly noticeable when you are newly in love/lust and you and your boyfriend of the moment have actually managed to put on some clothes to rejoin civilization for a meal out together. So there you two lovebirds are, pawing each other and giggling in a way that makes others (even the waiters) hate you, when you notice this couple a few tables down who are just quietly trying to eat their meal. This is the point where you, drunk and obnoxious on love/lust, whisper to your soul mate of the hour, "Sheesh, I hope we're never like that couple over there, the ones who aren't talking to each other. How depressing." And when you say it, you of course have to point to them as well, which is of course so incredibly rude, but you don't care because your hunky new boyfriend thinks everything you do is cute (honey, enjoy it, it doesn't last). I know this all too well, because I was once that annoying girl in love, and I would always notice those couples.

What goes around, comes around.

Yup. You guessed it, so now there I was, sitting in the restaurant and I was part of the depressing nontalking couple, and I actually overheard the love/lust couple a few tables down from us talking the very same trash about me, or rather us. (How could I not, she had the voice of a baboon.) I felt awful. Actually, I felt worse than that, because not only were my feelings hurt by some complete stranger who really should learn to mind her own damn business and should just concentrate on her own relationship (I noticed her boyfriend checking out one of the waitresses when she was in the bathroom. So there.), but I also felt ashamed that I had been the finger-pointer in the past, and probably made some other women feel like dirt. (Please accept my apologies; men really make us do dumb things.) And continuing full circle I want to add that I also felt bad for them, too, because they really had no idea how difficult it was to keep a relationship going once that oogly-googly stuff starts to fade (and it always fades), and so one day in the future, if they make it to Year 4 of married life, they might understand that sometimes you just don't have much to say when eating lunch together for the five thousandth time. But most of all, I felt for my husband, who had no idea that any of this was going on and just seemed pretty happy with his hamburger.

So suddenly I'm all mad and sad and confused and wondering how on earth I happen to be living through this cosmic life lesson, and instead of talking about it with my husband, I decide instead to feel sorry for myself and to wonder whether there is in fact something wrong with my marriage that is making us be that couple that I never wanted, nor expected, to be. This leads me down the road of marriage being difficult, and then me feeling bratty that I expect it to be easy, and then back to me wondering if there's a problem with our marriage since it is so difficult (maybe the cliché people are just wrong and it's not supposed to be hard work, because after all, love is pretty damn easy in the beginning, so it doesn't really make sense that it would get to be so hard later on), and then suddenly we are paying the check and the next thing you know I'm rolling my eyes about having to go into yet another freakin' antiques store. I DON'T LIKE OLD USED STUFF!

So I'm all sulky and hating my life and doing that five-year-old thing where I'm dragging my feet around the store and sticking out my bottom lip in a big old pout (and not the sexy kind either), and I see this typewriter and I walk over to it, and then I wonder whether the piece of paper sticking in it is an indicator that it works and decide to test it. Instead of typing the sentence that uses every letter in the alphabet that they teach you in typing class to learn where all the keys are (i.e., "See the quick brown fox jump over the lazy dog"), I end up typing my exact sentiment of the moment. . . . And now we're all caught up.

Cosmas sees what I wrote and scowls and then gives me a really hurt look with mean sprinkles and then he stalks out of the store. I, continuing on my odyssey to be named the dumbest person alive, go after him with the intention of trying to explain, but honestly, I should have known better, because there is really no good explanation for what I wrote, now, is there? And since I'm already worked up—I, of course, just make everything worse and suddenly we are in one of those raging sidewalk fights where people can't help but stare. Somehow we eventually make it home, but by that time we are no longer speaking to each other, not in the passive way like in the diner, but in the really aggressive way that couples do when they are just too angry to even bother.

I am now in the bedroom under the covers and he is sitting on the couch in the living room. I'm still really, really mad, mainly mad at myself, but also a little mad at him from the sidewalk where we both said a few things that I don't care to repeat because they are the run-of-the-mill mean things that married people sometimes say to each other in times of frustration. After being married for a while it's true that you start to pick up a secret language where you really can communicate on a whole new level because of how close you have become, but at the same time you also learn a few lessons on how to really and truly piss off the other person.

These times of self-loathing really make you take stock of your life, and also make you feel that getting older and wiser sometimes sucks. Life experience is surely a good thing, but it can also be hard to swallow. This makes you remember that you really didn't eat that much for lunch due to the stupid couple that made you feel bad about yourself earlier, and it also makes you remember the fact that your husband didn't get to eat any dessert because you pretty much became an ice queen by the end of the meal, so much so that he realized it was better to just get the check.

Suddenly, you are filled with the urge to fix all that has just gone wrong in the previous few hours, and though you know that you can't really fix anything (if only it were a matter of a little tube of cement glue), you do know that you can soothe away some of the rough edges if you really try. Remember Bactine, that spray stuff that your mom would put on your boo-boos when you were little? Those scraped knees and elbows, that gash on your finger you got from sticking your finger into the spokes of your tricycle. Yes, Bactine was the greatest, and I have my suspicions that it wasn't really very medicinal at all, but somehow it just made you feel better. That's what I need now, a kind of Bactine equivalent for the little "scrape" that I had gotten in, something to make us at least feel better.

It comes to me in a flash—not a flash of light (I mean, I'm not claiming to have been visited by an angel or anything)—just that little spark of an idea in your brain when you feel that you have just come up with the perfect idea that won't save the world, but just might save this day.

Pie.

What he needs and what I need is pie! I mean if you look back in time I'd be willing to bet that a lot of great things have happened over pie—people have fallen in love, families have bonded over the holidays, bank robbers have celebrated, and even a few loner types have felt better about their lives for those glorious eight minutes when they are eating a piece of pie. I'm a big believer that if everyone had a piece of pie every day then there would be a lot less cranky people (well, okay, for us gals who are weight obsessed, maybe a piece of pie a month?), mainly because it's really difficult to be mean and hateful over pie, am I right?

I'm out the door before he even has time to ask where I'm going (the only thing better than regular pie is surprise pie), but I'm not gone very long, as I head straight to a new pie shop that has opened near our house. Only fifteen minutes later I'm walking through the door with a three-berry pie (blueberry, raspberry, blackberry) and a cup full of homemade whipped cream; hell, with the whipped cream I might even get lucky and get a little make-up sex. When I announce that I come bearing pie I don't really get the response that I hoped for, but I do see a flicker of pie surprise move across his face. I let him know that it's totally fresh and even a bit warm, and he plays hard to get by saying that he prefers his pie cold. Fine, I deserve the snarkiness, but I will not be deterred. I ignore his comment and just begin to cut and serve.

In the kitchen I can't help but wonder whether the pie will negate my need to make a formal apology (if they would have had cherry pie, his favorite, I definitely wouldn't have had to do both). I decide to give him some extra whipped cream and just play it loose. After all, the fight at its very core wasn't really between me and Cosmas, but was more between me and my own viewpoint on marriage. Perhaps one of the reasons that marriage is so difficult is because it's hard to ignore the preconceived notions that everyone has about it (honestly, maybe everyone should keep their negative opinions to themselves). And perhaps one of the reasons marriage feels so long is because it takes a long time to figure it out, if such a thing is even possible. (What do I know, I've only been married four years.)

While we eat pie, we don't speak. The small lesson of the day is that sometimes it might not be so bad to be that couple who doesn't have to talk. Marriage is stupid sometimes, and, yes, sometimes so am I.

LIFE LESSONS
WRAPPED IN WONTONS

Just when I thought I had reached all the different levels of mother-daughter hell (e.g., Level 4: I-just-don't-understand-why-you're-not-having-a-baby-yet-what-does-that-mean-that-you-don't-know-if-you're-ready-what-does-that-matter-when-I'm-ready-to-be-a-grandmother-and-did-I-mention-that-Mrs. K.-at-church-has-four-grandchildren-already-and-that-every-week-I-have-to-look-at-more-pictures-I-want-to-show-some-pictures-of-my-own-where-are-my-pictures?-you-really-are-being-selfish-don't-you-think? [I honestly thought it would end once my brother had a baby, but in a weird way it only made it worse]), just when I thought I had witnessed it all (i.e., the fights, the tantrums, the frenzied drive to the mall for a few Godiva chocolate-covered strawberries that I chomp down while muttering that there are plenty worse daughters to have than me...), I find myself faced with a whole new situation that I'm not sure how to handle. My mom tells me that she's going to teach me how to make egg rolls.

Now, please note the word usage, as it's very important; my mom doesn't ask me if I would like to learn how to make egg rolls, she tells me in that mother voice that overrides the Constitution about everyone being free in this country, because it's not true. Ha. I'm not free, and I know it, but is any daughter really free when it comes to her mother?

So now I'm wondering whether my mom has temporarily forgotten that even though I'm technically Korean, I was born and raised in Tennessee, which happens to be in the United States of America, and never mind the fact that I'm thirty-three years old and not particularly fond of cooking (which is probably a textbook psychological reaction to the fact that I grew up in a house where I watched my mother make three meals a day for her husband and children— every damn day—and it seemed like she was always in the kitchen either cooking or cleaning up from cooking).

Forget all that bunk about people suppressing the really horrible things that happen in their lives, as I have total recall when it comes to my mom's first visit to my first real apartment. I was living in New York City on Thirtieth Street between Second and Third Avenues in a pretty sweet two-bedroom apartment that I shared with my friend Jane. In preparation for her visit I cleaned for days, and we're not talking just light surface stuff, but serious oh-my-God-she's-going-to-be-here-soon deep cleaning. That little ridge on the baseboard—dusted it. The blue plastic silverware caddy (did you know it was called a caddy? I just found out myself); went through the dishwasher. I even risked life and limb by climbing out on my rickety fire escape to clean the outside windows (well, I was also making sure that it was stable enough to hold my weight in the middle of the night to smoke that secret cigarette after she went to sleep).

So after picking her up at La Guardia Airport and bringing her into my superclean abode I remember walking in with the bravado of a twenty-two-year-old who was thinking she was on par with Ralph Macchio from *The Karate Kid* and thinking that the student had become the master. I watched as her eyes scanned the gleaming kitchen (I had even cleaned the handles on the kitchen cabinets, as well as the space on the fridge behind the handle where pesky dirt can hide)—so far so good. Next we moved down the hall to my bedroom, which was cluttered with books, but still pretty presentable, especially since I had made my bed for the first time since leaving home for college almost five years ago. She then excused herself to the bathroom and I stood out in the hallway imagining her opening the medicine cabinet (everything was arranged in order of height), lifting up the seat on the toilet to make sure that the rim was clean (yeah, like I'd be caught making such a rookie mistake), and if she took the time to pull back the shower curtain she would even be able to see that the soap was not lying in soapy water in the soap tray; no, I had cleaned that too.

The final frontier was the living room, which was the biggest challenge, since it was southern exposure and nothing shows dust like a sunny day. Not being able to help myself, I said, "Sooooo, whaddya think?" She gave me a small smile (SCORE!) and then promptly went back into the kitchen and tore off a paper towel and wet it in the sink. UH-OH. WHAT WAS SHE DOING? WHY DID SHE NEED A DAMP PAPER TOWEL? DAMP PAPER TOWELS WERE NEVER A GOOD THING.

She then walked back into the living room and walked over to the TV and proceeded to wipe down the screen. When she pulled back her hand, the paper towel was now filthy, basically black with the standard smut that came through the windows when you lived in a major metropolitan city. She must have noticed the suicidal look on my face and was nice enough to not comment, but it didn't matter, the damage was done, seared forever in my brain and filed under "Why My Mother Makes Me Crazy."

I was young then, and now I'm older by ten years or so and you would think that a visit from my mom wouldn't be so traumatic anymore, especially since I'm now married and no longer have to rely on her to send me an extra two hundred bucks a month so my electricity won't get turned off. You would think, right?

So on the fourth day of my mom's current visit, when she announced that she wanted to teach me how to make egg rolls, I did what any grown daughter would do in a similar situation. I said, "Yes, Mom." (That's "wimp" with a capital *W*, thank you very much.)

We headed to the local Asian food market and I skulked around the store staring at packets of freeze-dried God only knows what (I can't read Korean, so your guess is as good as mine) while my mom whooped it up with the female store owner. Yeah, there they were laughing away, and I couldn't help but be jealous that my mom gave all her charm away to strangers. We never laughed like that. Okay, we have, but never when it came to cooking or cleaning. I imagined them talking about the "young people of today" and I was certain that my mom was telling this woman that her own daughter, who was thirty-three years old, didn't know how to make egg rolls (or babies, but that was a whole other tale of woe that would best be saved for later); I mean honestly, what was the world coming to? The store owner gave my mom lots of sympathetic clucking in return; she's no dummy, she knew a big sale was coming.

Since my current cabinet was pretty bare, we had to buy everything: Chinese cabbage, fresh garlic (my mom didn't cheat like I did by using the prechopped stuff they sold in jars), scallions, ground pork, ground beef, rice noodles, shitake mushrooms, bamboo, wonton skins, eggs, and a bunch of spices.

For the next six hours—that's right, SIX HOURS—we slaved away in my tiny galley kitchen. Since the only way to really learn how to make egg rolls was to do them yourself, I did the majority of the chopping, dicing, slicing (which are all different, in case you didn't know), sautéing, and I washed the same skillet over and over and over. What makes egg-roll making so tedious is that every single ingredient must be cooked separately and put aside to be mixed together at the end. Now, why this is necessary, I can't tell you, and believe me, I asked, I cajoled, I begged my mom to try to find some shortcuts, but she said, No. No. No. Supposedly, if you cooked everything together all the different flavors would mix together in a way that was vastly different from the way all the flavors would mix together WHEN WE LATER MIXED EVERYTHING TOGETHER AND PUT THEM INTO LITTLE WONTON SKINS. YEAH, LIKE THAT REALLY MAKES SENSE, BUT WHATEVER.

This was so not the Joy Luck Club. By Hour 4 I had pretty much thought about all the ways I could off myself while making egg rolls (sticking metal chopstick in outlet, tossing match into bubbling wok oil, mixing up stuff prematurely and having my mom kill me). And while washing my nonstick All-Clad pan for the eighteenth time, I reached my breaking point.

"Why do I have to learn how to make egg rolls?"

My mom seemed surprised by my question, or maybe she was just surprised by my tone—it was the tone of a woman who was about to start bawling.

"What? You didn't want to learn?" One thing that I really appreciate about my mom is that she really plays clueless well. I mean, nobody does it better.

"Did I say I wanted to learn? Did you hear me say, 'Mom, oh Mom, please, please teach me how to make egg rolls'?"

She hates when I get sarcastic, and she frowned with disapproval. "Is it so bad to learn how to make egg rolls?"

Well, she had me there. Because truth be told, it wasn't so bad, and the only reason I was miserable was because I was making myself miserable.

"You have a bad attitude."

I was no longer seven years old, so I felt like I could respond. "Oh yeah? You're bossy."

"Why do you make everything so difficult for yourself?"

"Why do you make everything so difficult for me?"

"I'm not difficult."

I could not stop myself, I laughed. But I stopped quickly, as I knew I had hurt her feelings. I tried to keep my anger going, because, well, because otherwise I'd soon be apologizing and then later after she left I'd be so mad at myself for giving in, for not speaking up. Why was it so damn hard for me to communicate with her? What is it about mothers that makes you so crazy?

"Forget it. Let's just finish." And we didn't really speak for the last two hours, which were spent at the kitchen table assembling the egg rolls one by one. I had gotten out a little of my pent-up frustration, so I was a little more relaxed now, and I actually liked this part of the drill. This was the part that I already knew how to do, because while growing up, this was the part she always let me help her with. When I was little I wasn't that precise, and I know I annoyed her by not making them all the same size and shape. Some of mine were too skinny. Some were too fat. Some I didn't close properly, so when they were fried in the oil they would break apart and Mom would have to stop everything and fish out all the little pieces and start again. I do remember she didn't give me a hard time about it, which I guess was because I was young.

Now I was older, and I was much more detail-oriented in general. In fact, perhaps I was a little too precise, because my mom rolled two up in the time that it took me to finish one. Soon we had a pretty decent pile of them for our efforts, and I couldn't help but be pleased that I had something to show for my now lost day.

While I was watching over the ones that were frying in the wok (finally, we were at the end), I thought about the fact that we had egg rolls a lot growing up. We all loved them, and because my mom loved us, she gave away countless afternoons of her own time to stand in the kitchen for six hours and make them for us. I do recall asking her once why it took so long to make egg rolls and how she had the patience to cook for so long. She told me that anything good requires effort, and that just because something was difficult didn't make it bad.

I have a difficult relationship with my mom, and I know that a lot of it is my own doing. I feel like she's too critical. I feel like she pressures me. I feel like she doesn't ever take the time to really understand me. But maybe, and I'm not totally conceding here, maybe our relationship isn't quite as fraught with strife as I think it is. In the past six hours I have learned two lessons in life thanks to my mom: I have learned how to make egg rolls. And I have learned that just because something is difficult doesn't make it bad.

C'MON, EVERYONE IS DOING IT

One of the perks of actually surviving our years in school is that we should no longer have to deal with peer pressure. No more looking down at our feet when our friends are goading us to do drugs, lose our virginity, or in my case, share homework. (Yes, we honor-roll students got pressured too!) I will say that I was not the type to cave in to pressure from my friends on such things, and on more than one occasion I might have actually been the one subtly applying the pressure *(C'mon, every teenager sneaks out of the house at night and "borrows" the family car....)*, but it's all water under the bridge. I mean, thank God, we're past that stage of our lives, right?!

Yeah, I wish.

So I'm sitting at a table with a few friends and everyone is feeling the belly of our one very pregnant friend. Our superstomached friend is enjoying the attention, or perhaps what she's really enjoying is that third slice of banana bread that she gets to eat while the rest of us are stuck drinking nonfat, nonsweetened, nontaste lattes while considering that pregnancy may not be so bad after all if it gives you license to eat three servings of anything.

I am not joining in on the belly rubbing, as my hands are currently by my side, gripping the side of my chair so they don't grab at the fourth slice of banana bread, which is sitting smugly on the plate in front of me going "Nyah, nyah, you've never tasted a carb so good." But even if I weren't currently being tempted to grab the fourth slice of banana bread and shove it whole into my mouth while no one was looking, I knew that I still probably wouldn't be touching the belly-of-life that is before me.

I have never touched a pregnant belly, well, not really, not in the way most other women do, where they ooh and aah and make a big show of guessing the sex of the child (geez, I mean with odds of fifty-fifty, it's not such a big deal). My best friend, Laura, let me poke at her pregnant belly once when I asked to, but it was more that I wanted physical proof that she was actually "with child" when it seemed that just hours ago we were still college roommates wolfing down lo mein at our favorite Chinese restaurant before running back to the dorm to watch the newest installment of *90210* (when Shannen Doherty was still on the show). It's not that I'm scared of touching one; I'm terrified of it.

Irrational? Maybe. Squeamish? No. Freaked out that there is a living creature that is currently residing in the only place smaller than a Manhattan apartment? Absolutely.

Obviously, I'm freaked out because the whole thing is totally bizarre when you really think about it. I mean I'm all for growing up, getting older, getting wiser, and all that, but I have very mixed feelings about making my body a landlord for a tenant whom I don't know and who will inherit half of my genes—the same genes that made me really hyper, really wild, and the type of person who thought sneaking out in the middle of the night to ride around in "borrowed" parents' cars was really cool.

This is when I wake up from my reverie to my friends telling me that perhaps I should take off the plastic wrap from the banana bread before trying to eat it.

I put down the banana bread that I didn't even realize I was holding (see what happens when you let go of the chair?) and shake my head. "No, of course, I don't really want it. Carbs are bad." And I watch as the giant stomach with arms nonchalantly takes it while throwing out the "eating for two" excuse, which would be equivalent to a royal flush if we were playing poker.

After demolishing my slice (I say "my" because my fingerprints were on the wrapper that once held it), the stomach speaks to me, and when the stomach speaks everyone listens.

"So, Jenny, when is it your turn?"

Well, if we're talking about when it's my turn to eat banana bread, the answer is obviously not when you're around, but I don't say that. I don't say anything.

My silence is taken for shyness, which is funny, because I'm not shy. No, I'm loud. I'm surprisingly vulgar at times. And I'm definitely not going to go down this road of conversation.

The stomach speaks again. "You two have been married for how many years now?"

In my mind I add up the years I've been shackled in marriage, and with a little quick thinking I say, "Twenty-eight in dog years."

This gets a lot of laughs and one of the nonstomach girls takes the bait and begins to talk about her dog and I can almost smell the freedom of a last-minute subject change, but the stomach will not be deterred.

"Four years? What are you waiting for?"

This stomach, in its smaller, less annoying state, has once lived in New York and knows that I too have once called New York my home, which means that it knows how to cut to the chase and just be direct. Very direct. Yes, the stomach is right, it has been four years of marriage, and I'm pleased to say that having been four years without children is actually not the worst place to be, because when most people who don't know you hear that you have been married four years and still don't have a fat baby in your arms, they come to the natural conclusion that maybe there is a problem (because who in their right mind would want to wait so long to show off a fat baby?) and they pretty much don't tend to grill you for fear that you might break down crying over all the problems you've had, and while they are nosy enough to feel they have license to judge all the choices you make in life, what they don't want is to hear about one woman's problems with fertility.

I have no problems with fertility. (Well, as far as I know. Knock on wood.)

This is the point where I would look down at my feet, but I can't because I'm sitting down and can't see them. So instead I trace the grain in the wood on the table before me. "We're not waiting for anything in particular. But we've been talking about it a lot more recently." Ha. My new plan is to throw the stomach a bone; maybe that will temporarily give the eating machine pause while I try to make a getaway.

The stomach has no use for bones (probably because it is satiated with four pieces of banana bread) and pushes forward. "I'm not sure if you've heard, but last time I checked, talking won't make a baby."

The whole table erupts in laughter at this one, and the table even moves as the stomach is shaking over its own fabulous wit. I throw a couple of mean looks at the other non-stomach girls at the table, but one replies with a small smile that says, *Ha-ha, finally, being over thirty and single comes in handy,* and the other nonstomach is a lesbian. (Man, if ever there was a time I wished I were a lesbian, it was now.)

"C'mon, it would be so great if you were pregnant. I mean, it's really the most wonderful thing ever. I really think you should try it." (Insert pregnant pause here.) "Everyone is doing it."

This is where I want to stand up and yell out, "Objection!" Because truth be told, we are surrounded by lots of people in a coffee shop and there are no other bully bellies in the room, just one.

Instead, I contemplate the fact that my brother and his wife have a baby, that half of my friends are pregnant or have already had their first baby, and some are even starting to steel themselves for Round 2, and that even *Us Weekly* regularly features "bump alerts" of the stars.

Maybe the stomach is right. Maybe it is time to face my fears (nine months with no control over my own body) and instead look at the positives (all the banana bread you can eat) that come with being on the pregnancy track. I mean so what that I could never again go to an opening movie night. So what that I could no longer afford to buy slinky over-priced sandals. So what that I couldn't come and go as I please (well, almost—I do have a dog who sulks whenever left behind); I mean honestly, I'm not even going anywhere all that exciting anymore. I'm no longer going to dance clubs. I'm no longer closing down bars. I'm no longer taking last-minute trips to Paris (actually, I had never taken a last-minute trip to Paris, but I like knowing that I could if I wanted to).

The stomach is silent, because it knows that it has been successful. Thirty-something peer pressure is different from teenage peer pressure, in that it doesn't need instant gratification. No, thirty-something peer pressure is craftier than that, as it knows that the best way to get people on board is to plant a few seeds and to let nature take its course (yes, I'm aware this metaphor is overkill), and soon enough I'll be my own worst enemy.

I take a deep breath, trying to clear my head. I mean, jumping on board the pregnancy platform isn't something I can do right then and there anyway (I can never properly think about sex when in the presence of baked goods for sale).

I try not to feel bad about the whole thing; I mean after all, the stomach is bigger than me. It's bigger than us all.

AN AFFAIR TO FORGET

I am thinking about having affairs, which, mind you, is different from thinking about actually having an affair *myself,* which I'm not all that interested in, as it probably requires the purchase of new underwear (the only kind of shopping I hate to do). What I've been thinking is that in books, movies, and the random gossip you hear, it seems that lots of people have affairs; in fact, I think I heard somewhere that the number of women who have affairs is anywhere from fifteen to sixty-five percent (people apparently lie a lot about this type of thing, and it's hard to get an actual number, so let's split the difference and say forty percent). Anyway, supposedly the number one reason that women have affairs is that they feel like they are being taken for granted by their husbands. And if the statistic surprises me, the reason certainly doesn't. At all.

Not that my husband necessarily takes me for granted; after all, being the workaholic type, he's not home enough to do so. So I am often left alone to contemplate things like my weight, the fact that I have a lot of gray hair coming in, the fact that I have a blister on my heel that won't seem to heal, prompting me to wonder whether I have some sneaky disease that will soon kill me, and whether my lips are always chapped now because I've actually become addicted to Burt's Beeswax lip balm. Oh yeah, and every now and again I think about people who have affairs.

First off, what I want to know is whether these women who have affairs just wake up one morning and decide to have an affair (*I really don't feel like going to the gym today, hmmmm, maybe I'll succumb to someone's arts of seduction*), or whether it just sort of happens by accident, like when you trip on the sidewalk over absolutely nothing and feel like an idiot. I suppose it's nicer just to give everyone the benefit of the doubt and assume that it mainly happens by accident. Like, there she was minding her own business at the local Starbucks—reading the paper, wearing some low-cut sexy blouse, and smiling at anyone with testosterone—oh, and now she's having an affair. Oops, how'd that happen?

No, but seriously, I'm a big fan of *Terms of Endearment*, and I remember thinking that when Debra Winger's character is being humiliated at the supermarket for lack of funds by the mean cash-register lady and the sweet-hearted John Lithgow comes to her rescue, that it seemed like a very real

moment. From what I've read, a lot of affairs start when
two people who both have "needs" that are currently unfulfilled (again, benefit of doubt, let's assume for both the
needs are emotional and not sexual) happen to meet. So
Debra needed cash and was not so thrilled with her life at
the moment, and John had cash and he was lonely. Frankly,
I sympathized with them both (though not her husband,
Skip, as he had totally been cheating on Debra already and
with his own students, for Christ's sake. Bad Skip).

Indeed, in view of my own unfulfilled needs of late, I
can understand how it happens. (Sorry, I'm not about to
confess some secret liaison with my mailman, though he
does tend to ask me about my day, which is more than I can
generally say about my husband.) I mean if I met some guy
who was just dying to take out someone's trash every day
(without ever forgetting), who also happened to be tall
(which would help him change lightbulbs in a prompt and
timely manner), and maybe even lived for carrying gro-
ceries up three flights of stairs once a week, then perhaps I,
too, could find myself stumbling headlong into an affair.
Though honestly, what's the likelihood of me just running
into such a man (or such a man even existing), right?

So let me flip the scenario and ponder the sort of
woman who might meet my husband's unfulfilled needs.
Hmmmm…she would need to be a woman who didn't get
mad about day-old trash, someone who didn't have much
use for light, and someone who thinks of huffing grocery
bags as a great cardio workout. I don't know. What *might*
my husband's unfulfilled needs be?…

When I call Cosmas at work, I can tell that he's busy. But since he forgot to take the trash out (AGAIN) this morning, I also know perfectly well that I have the upper hand.

I start sweet. "Honeybear, do you have a second to talk?"

He answers me in that beleaguered-husband tone that I hate. "I'm sorry I forgot the trash."

"Oh, that's okay. I'm not calling about that."

"Oh?" Now I've piqued his curiosity; anything that's on my mind that takes a backseat to the trash is probably worth listening to.

"So, I was wondering whether you have any unfulfilled needs you might want to tell me about." And then I go on to explain how unfulfilled needs was a biggie on the reasons-why-people-have-affairs list. (Though I still tend to think the number one reason that men have affairs is because they want sex.) Cosmas is of course used to these random questions from me, so when he answers it's in his why-does-my-wife-call-me-with-such-random-questions voice.

"Do you think we can talk about this later when I get home?"

I consider his request and decide that yes, perhaps a face-to-face conversation might be better when it comes to questioning if my husband may or may not have some major hankering that is currently unfulfilled—and that may propel him, at any moment, to meet some loose woman down at our local Starbucks.

By the time he gets home from work that night I'm already ensconced with the TV (I assume there isn't a huge

rush to figure this out now since he has come home to me after all, right?), and the subject doesn't come up until we're
getting ready for bed. The odd thing is, he's the one who
brings it up.

"So, what was with your phone call today?"

I find myself suddenly nervous that he's desperately
been looking for a way to confess some dark lurking secret
to me for a while now, and since I've actually had the temer-
ity to ask, he's about to throw out some sort of ultimatum
that involves my addressing his unfulfilled needs for a wife
who wears slinky lingerie, or else. Which would be a
dilemma; I mean, if someone wants to explain how you are
supposed to sleep in lingerie without having it bunch up,
please do... (though perhaps the whole point of lingerie
isn't the sleeping, eh?).

When in doubt, do the denial thing.

"What are you talking about?" I ask innocently enough.
"I didn't call you today." (Advice: When doing the denial
thing, do it better than that.)

"Yes you did." Now he's sort of squinting at me in a
weird, suspicious way.

Should I keep up with the bad lying? "Oh, *that* phone
call. Right. Now I remember." I give him a fake yawn, as if
to dismiss the whole thing. Why, oh, why am I such a trou-
blemaker? I really should not be left alone during the day.

He lets it go, and we both climb into bed. But I can't
sleep, and after a few minutes I grab his shoulder and start
shaking. (Cosmas can fall asleep instantly.)

"So, do you?" I ask softly. That's the best thing about being in the dark—it's easier to deal with bad news because no one can see facial expressions.

"Nope."

Wow, sometimes I really envy men for their ability to see things in black or white. I decide to quit while I'm ahead.

The next morning Cosmas changes all the lightbulbs that are out in the apartment, and then he takes out the trash, but not before giving me a big kiss on the cheek. And so I adjust my own list of unfulfilled needs accordingly.

But once he's left for work and I'm all alone again, I can't help thinking about affairs again. I wonder if one of the requirements for having an affair is a big trench coat to wear while you're sneaking around (though, to be honest, I've always thought wearing a trench coat makes a person more noticeable than not). Now, I'm not saying that everyone who wears a trench coat is necessarily on the way to a tryst (or even to deliver secret government documents), but I do think that one of the most obvious things you can do to not get caught while cheating is to dress the way you normally would.

Aha, I think to myself. I bet the reason why no one has ever approached me to have an affair with is because I probably don't look like a woman who would be fun to have an affair with. I mean, most days I'm in jeans and a T-shirt, and it's a good day if my hair doesn't look like I just woke up. I suppose that if I were a guy who was sniffing around for an affair (by accident, of course), I'd probably be less inclined to start chatting me up at Starbucks than some sexy vixen who knows how to drink her nonfat nontaste latte without losing her lipstick.

I mean if we were to look at a cheating-is-bad movie, *Unfaithful,* with Richard Gere and Diane Lane (who, for the record, my husband would leave me for in a New York minute), the husband figured out that his wife was cheating solely by the fact that she was wearing expensive shoes and wearing lots of high-end underwear. Of course, he could have figured it out earlier if he'd just paid attention to her guilty smile and the fact that she was humming around the house. (Women, as a rule, do not hum around the house while doing housework, and if you know any women who do, then I'm willing to bet that they're falling somewhere in that forty percent.)

This new line of thinking leads me to wonder if my own husband would even notice if I were to start behaving this way—you know, shaving my legs more regularly, making up random excuses to go to the store and then disappearing for an hour or more, and maybe even doing a little humming of my own (while I'm waiting for the microwave to finish warming up our dinners). Of course, I know that this was a bad idea right away, but like most bad ideas, it does have a certain appeal.

I mean, when you really think about infidelity, it's probably more trouble than it's worth. Fine, so maybe you get some great sex and a guy who finds every word you say completely fascinating, but hopefully most of us had that at the beginning of our relationship with our husbands, and we all know that it doesn't last. And the consequences of an affair coming to light—the hurt feelings, the rage, the fights, the shame, and all that expensive new lingerie going to waste—would it really be worth it? Maybe a better way to relieve boredom is to start going to see matinee movies by yourself instead (and then you can simply cheat on your *diet* by actually getting a little butter on your popcorn, which is almost as high on the sin list)....

Cosmas usually calls me midday, and as I'm digging frantically through my purse trying to unearth my phone I decide at the last minute not to answer it. He hates to leave messages, and so after twenty minutes I watch as my phone rings again, taking a certain perverse pleasure in watching the word "husband" blinking on the LCD screen. Though we certainly don't have the kind of relationship where we have to report our every move to each other, I'm sure that he's mildly perplexed as to why I'm not answering. Normally, I'd tell him if I'm having lunch with a friend or running errands. By the end of the day he's called two more times, and the fifth time he calls, I start to worry that perhaps he actually needs me for some reason, so I pick up the phone.

"Hey, where've you been all day? I've been calling."

"Is something wrong?" I ask, because if something were wrong, I'd, of course, end my charade immediately.

"No, but it's just annoying that you didn't answer the phone." Bad move on his part. I could have had a legitimate reason not to answer my phone, so why be snarky about it?

"Oh, sorry. I was out."

"Out where?"

"Oh, y'know. Running errands."

"Did you finally remember to pick up my shirts at the cleaner?" This tone of voice isn't going to get him anywhere.

"No."

"Did you go to the grocery store? I was going to have cereal this morning, but we were out of milk."

"No."

"So, what errands did you run?"

"Geez, what's with the third degree? I just had a little of this and a little of that to do."

"I know you're hiding something." Wow, maybe he should give up his day job and become a P.I.

"What are you talking about? I'm not hiding anything."

"What did you buy?"

"What?"

"You're acting all weird because you went shopping and you bought something that you shouldn't have bought. I know you."

Hmmm, now I was in a dilemma. So am I a woman who is having an affair who doesn't want to get caught? Or am I a woman who is having an affair as a cry for help in her marriage? I tell him to hold on, while I muffle the phone and flip a coin.

"I wasn't out shopping and I didn't buy something I shouldn't have."

"Oh, okay. So you've just been out all day doing this and that."

"Yup."

"I see."

"Well, gotta go. I'm assuming you're still working late, right?"

"What makes you say that?"

"Oh, I don't know—because you said this morning that you were working late. Look, I'm not mad. It's fine. You can work late if you want to."

Now he's really suspicious. "Actually, I'm thinking about coming home to have dinner with my beautiful wife."

I try my best to sound sort of disappointed. But I'm not sure it's worked.

PARENTS ON BOARD?!

Lately, my husband, Cosmas, and I have been having an awful lot of conversations about the Cambridge public-school system for a couple who have no kids. Maybe it's because we live just a block and a half away from the Maria L. Baldwin elementary school, with all of its yellow school buses, car-pool drop-offs, and parents walking their kids to school in the mornings at precisely the time I'm out walking our dog. I can never get close enough to actually hear what these kids are chattering about (Wendell, our wheaten terrier, looks at small children as if they're unusually large squeaky toys meant to be chased down and barked at), but I listen to their high-pitched singsong voices and imagine them asking the questions that only small children are smart enough to ask:

Why *can't* they wear their favorite orange socks for the second day in a row if it makes them happy (surely little kids' feet don't *really* smell, right?). I like the way their parents respond by opening and closing their mouths, trying to come up with some answer that won't simply lead to another question, all the while wondering if they're being a little hypocritical, since they happen to be wearing a dirty pair of socks themselves.

Or perhaps we keep coming back to the school subject because we pass right by the Cambridge Rindge & Latin high school as I drive my husband to Mass General Hospital on the days he sees patients, or to his office at the Whitehead Genome Center when he spends his day with his "little patients," which is how I fondly refer to the cells and DNA samples he does his research on. Cosmas, being repetitive by nature (always wanting to go to the same restaurants to order exactly the same thing), always asks the same question: "How come none of these kids are ever carrying books?" I have to jump in quick at this point if I don't want to hear about his own high school experience, which seems to involve only homework, studying at the library, and reading back issues of *Scientific American*. Most of the time I just poke fun at him by pointing to the girl who does seem to be busy studying...what appears to be the new *Us Weekly*. Or I explain to him that perhaps schools have done away with books altogether after student complaints that there is *no way* they have time to talk on the phone with their friends while watching MTV *and* read.

Shaking his head balefully at my sarcasm on schedule, he then informs me that *our* future children will *not* have access to friends *or* television until after they've received their early acceptance letters from Harvard. Depending on my mood I then tease him about my plans to raise well-rounded, socially-conscious kids who want to be poets or anthropologists, letting him know that I'm socking away cash for a secret scholarship fund for our kids' college tuition just in case his threats of not paying for any major other than premed or mathematics happen to be true (I'm calling it the Never You Mind Stodgy Old Dad Because Mom Says You Can Be Whatever You Want Scholarship). Or, on the rare occasion when I'm feeling serious, I ask about his real views on the debate of public versus private education.

Normally these talks quickly fizzle out once I remind him that we're still DINKs (double income no kids), but now that we've passed our four-year anniversary, the topic of kids is starting to gain traction. The hard part is deciding whether such talks are natural manifestations of our own internal longings or stem from plausible rumors that our mothers have joined forces to plot an action plan that involves flying into Logan, storming our apartment, and threatening us with bodily harm if we don't get busy procreating.

I suppose we've run out the clock on the good old days of subtlety and tact—like how every few months I would

receive recent clippings about a thirty-something couple
spending their life savings on high-tech fertilization proce-
dures, whether old eggs produce children who score lower
on their SATs, and the fact that Ivy League schools are getting more and more selective in their admissions practices
every year that goes by. Each article was adorned with a
brightly colored Post-it that inevitably had "F.Y.I.! But NO
PRESSURE" written in all caps with too many exclamation
points and a happy face with a smile that looked suspi-
ciously close to a frustrated frown.

Sometimes I showed these little tokens to Cosmas, but
more often than not I just filed them away in a folder labeled
"Things to Do When We Have More Money" (this file also
contained write-ups of four-star resorts on tropical islands,
dog-eared pages from the Neiman Marcus home catalog,
and an article reporting that hiring a personal chef may be
cheaper than takeout).

The repeated excuses about our unstable financial state
seem to be losing their effectiveness, however, and my
mom's new response is to point out that *lots* of people with
huge credit-card debt are having babies every day, and, like
the MasterCard commercials say, you just can't put a price
on family. Disconcerting as it may be to have your mother
parroting corporate advertising slogans in her babylust, she
does have a point. I guess it *is* a bit tacky to reduce your future offspring to another column on an Excel spreadsheet,
or a sliver on your Quicken pie chart.

But to this day I do not understand how people in the
Midwest manage to own a house, two cars, *and* afford kids,

when Cosmas and I—two urban professionals with above-average earning potential (if not necessarily an above-average earning *reality*)—still find ourselves incredibly cash poor every few months. (Cosmas, of course, is quick to point out that Midwestern wives watched *Sex and the City* purely as entertainment, not some kind of home shopping catalog for four-hundred-dollar shoes.)

Every week on the way to our local video store we find ourselves drawn to the windows of the two realty offices on Mass Ave that post pictures of condos and houses for sale in the area. Our eyes dilate over things like washer/dryer in unit, built-in bookshelves, and even the smallest patch of outdoor concrete that we could call our own. Cosmas, having stronger math skills (I have none), always does the mortgage math, but each time, no matter how small the place, no matter if we even say the hell with outdoor space, he shakes his head. This is where I offer consolation, saying that I heard kids have to be at least five years old anyway before they can be trusted to work the washer/dryer or other major appliances. Cosmas nods and stays silent, but I know he's thinking exactly what I am: It is unlikely that we'd ever be able to afford to upgrade our living space and have kids at the same time. Maybe we can look into raising ficus trees.

I am well aware that my incessant need to make bad jokes about our future offspring is probably just another indicator that our flirtation with the idea of having kids is reaching new heights—something similar to the elementary school behavior of being mean to the object of one's affection (did boys really dip the pigtails of their crushes in inkwells?)....

I mean, now that I think about it, a few years ago we never even noticed kids out on the street at all, but now it's like they are everywhere. And hard as I try not to comment, I can't help myself. Like the time we were having brunch at Sonsie when we were seated next to a couple that was coaxing their high-chaired progeny to eat an omelette, and I found myself whispering across the table, "Who knew you actually had to feed *them*, too? So much for being able to afford appetizers anymore."

Cosmas laughed, but I could tell by his expression that he was wary of even discussing children, as perhaps my biological clock was setting up some sort of subconscious trap for him. He tried to do his part of denial-via-feigned-indifference, by responding that he wasn't sure whether he was quite ready to share his "chauffeur" with anyone else, even if it was for tumbling-tot class.

Okay, forget the fact that I still have no clue how he even picked *up* the term "tumbling-tot class," or the fact that I, too, happened to know what this entailed. Let's just move on to my husband's inability to think ahead to whether his joke was appropriately targeted for its audience. You would think he'd have learned this skill by now after lots of bad backfire experience. But no—this time he actually topped himself by turning the gun on himself and firing directly. Truth be told, there is probably no way to refer to your wife as a chauffeur and have her find it amusing (well, unless she actually happened to *be* a chauffeur, which I am not).

In fact, one of my biggest irrational issues of even having kids comes down to not wanting to spend the better part of my day in a car. As it is, I'm already irritated that a precedent has been set where I drive Cosmas to and from work every day. Every now and again I try to make him take the T, explaining that the ten-minute walk to our house from Harvard Square would be good exercise, but somehow I always get that call where he doesn't have a coat, or his bag is really heavy, and he's willing to make dinner and do the dishes if only I pick him up. I always give in, as it is never more than twenty minutes round-trip (plus, Wendell loves car rides), but the idea of having to deal with a series of multiple stops, all the while listening to singing Muppets, is not something I care to think about.

I once made the mistake of referring to myself as Cosmas's "soccer mom" to my sister-in-law who actually happens to be a card-carrying soccer mom of two young boys, and she kindly set my ignorance straight by sharing with me what her weekdays involve. . . . How anyone in that household ever has time to sleep, I have no idea. By the end of the call I was near-catatonic from a headache of epic proportions—one that left Cosmas hard up for a good two weeks, I assure you.

I have read that couples who put off having kids for a while do have a harder time jumping on the red wagon, even once they have their finances in order. After all, it's easy to get set in your ways—eating sushi twice a week, always seeing two movies every weekend, and being able to actually sleep in for as long as the dog's bladder can stand. And why change a good thing, right?

But isn't it obvious that these conversations about public

schools, discussions of where we might be able to live, and the fact that I made sure our new car had a six-CD front-loading CD changer are all, in fact, "signs" leading us to the next big step (or, as the case may be, lots of *little* steps) in our lives? Maybe it *is* time that we have kids. But it's so hard to tell, because whenever we come in direct contact with couples our age who do have kids, I swear that they are always giving us opposing signals. It's something in the strangulated way they say, "Well, even though you may want something, sugarkins, doesn't mean you always get to *have* it, because, as you know, Mommy always wants a few minutes of quiet to enjoy her latte, but she doesn't always get *that*, now, does she?" Or the way they tell us point-blank that it's not the financial readiness that we should concern ourselves with, but whether we're really ready to give up our *freedom* and *sanity* for the-most-fulfilling-experience-of-our-lives.

In keeping with our new resolution to try being grown-ups every now and again, Cosmas and I finally sat down and had a conversation about having children. After a lot of very "adult" debate, we both realized that we very much want to have a family, but that we owe it to our future kids, really, to do a few more months—if not even, say, another year—of research into the studies of early elementary education in the Boston area.

It's what any good parent would do.

"SINGLE"

I have never been single in Boston, having moved here three years ago after surprising all my New York single friends and actually getting married (though the move to Boston might have been the bigger surprise). Though if you want to get picky I did attend Harvard for one glorious curfew-free summer in high school (1988), but teenage girls don't really refer to themselves as single anyway, right? And if you want to get really picky I guess you can say I wasn't even officially "single," but having my husband out of town on a five-day business trip without me for the first time, well, it was pretty close.

With my flexible schedule as a writer, coupled with the fact that my husband hated to be alone when he wasn't working, I would normally accompany him on business trips, but not this time. This time when he informed me that he had to go to Kiel, Germany, to pick up "wet" samples of DNA for his lab work, he made the mistake of tacking me on to the trip in such a way that I became slightly offended.

The trip actually was falling close enough to our anniversary and my birthday that if he had been smarter he could have gotten away with making the whole thing a "combo" gift (which I strictly forbade in the past, because it was never my idea to get married so close to my birthday, as I preferred to have my gifts evenly distributed throughout the year, so he was under strict orders that "combo" gifts were never allowed unless they were over-the-top romantic). So whereas he could have presented it as an exotic and celebratory trip abroad to the Baltic Sea (and-oh-by-the-way-since-we're-in-the-neighborhood-I-might-just-swing-by-the-German-lab-I'm-collaborating-with-to-pick-up-a-few-things), he presented it along the lines of "I have to go to Kiel to pick up some samples for work, and if you want to come along it would be a pretty cheap trip." It doesn't get any more unromantic than that. After I accused him of reducing me to basically a Post-it on a work file, he made his second mistake by laughing at my analogy and agreeing that it was sort of true. So, long story short, I told him to be sure to send me a postcard.

As I watched him pack the morning he was to leave, he kept reminding me that I could still change my mind and come along (he had actually purchased me a ticket, thinking that perhaps I was bluffing). I shook my head no, but told him that I was no longer upset about the whole thing (this was more out of paranoia that if his plane went down I didn't want to feel guilty for being a bitch the last time he saw me). What I didn't tell him was that I awoke that morning secretly excited by the prospect of being husbandless for the next five days. It's not like we had never been apart since we got married; in fact, we had been apart plenty, but normally it was I who was away from home, and I assumed that being alone on my home turf would be different.

I drove him to work, and as we hugged on the street he and I exchanged the standard "I love you" fares. I wished him a safe trip, and he told me to "be good." And when I responded in a coy and flirty voice that I hadn't used in years, "Oh, I'm always good," I suddenly felt a little ashamed. But after getting no more reaction from him than a distracted peck on the cheek, my guilt vanished. On the way home I blasted the stereo, and purposely left the volume on high even after I exited the car. (Cosmas hated getting in the car and having the music blast loud, so normally I was very conscientious about turning it down at the end of any solo driving experience.)

My first day alone was not really earth-shattering (because technically he wasn't even out of my zip code until later that evening), and the only thing to note was that I actually picked up things around the apartment more than I normally would. I attributed this to the fact that it was now my apartment for the next few days, and it was easier to keep it neat knowing there wouldn't be an outside force beyond my control (like a husband) to mess it up later.

The next morning, with my husband safely ensconced an ocean away, it was now time to work out my Saturday-night plans. I made a pact with myself that I would make sure that I was productive and did a lot of work for the next two days (so I could prove to Cosmas that I didn't need his presence to keep me in line) and then I would reward myself with two full days of when-the-cat's-away-those-mice-sure-do-play high jinks. Now all I needed was a partner in crime. The tricky part of being married, and more boring than not, was that a lot of my friends were in the exact same situation. In my head I went through all my friends here and in New York and one by one they got axed due to their kids, their pregnancy, or their work schedule. In the end, I was left with only two likely candidates—my neighbor and friend, Carrie (she was getting her master's at Harvard and I figured she might need to blow off a little steam before midterms), and one of my best friends (and only remaining single friend) in New York.

Jenner Sullivan was legendary in my life for being the most social person I knew. She had a crazy job that kept her jet-setting all over the world and I was always getting calls from Milan, Zurich, and the like—a quick catch-up session with her boring married friend via cell phone in between her meetings and expense-account international nightlife. When I finally got her assistant to put me through, Jenner informed me she had two minutes before she had to walk into a meeting so I had better talk fast.

I gave her the lowdown, telegram style—husband in Germany, Delta Shuttle, Saturday night in Boston, new bars and a bevy of New England's finest bachelors for her to test-drive any new flirting techniques on, and I promised to pay for brunch. She saw right through my pitch and asked, "What's in it for you?" It was here that I stammered, because truth be told, a "girls' night out" wouldn't rate superhigh on her social totem pole, but for me ... well, it was a chance to relive my glory days when I didn't even know what was on TV on Saturday nights. I told her that I'd never been "single" in quotations in Boston. I told her that I was in dire need of a fun girls' night out on the town with no curfew; and then I begged. She reminded me that if I was playing "single" (in quotations) in Boston, then by default Cosmas was "single" (in quotations) in Germany, though she added that she didn't think German women were really his type. Then she told me that she was willing and available, but that I should call her later once I gave some careful consideration to exactly why I felt like I needed a girls' night out so badly, and lastly she questioned how I'd feel after getting a taste of the life I had given up. Clearly, I had caught her after her weekly early-bird shrink appointment, so I told her where she could stuff her psychobabble, and that I'd call her later.

After I hung up the phone I was a bit disgruntled, not so much by her making fun of my pathetic desire to play "single" (I preferred the word "lame," myself), but more over her warning that I might regret digging up memories and feelings that might better be left in the past. Disgruntled quickly changed to defensive. Give me a break; was it so wrong to want to go out on the town when my husband was away? Of course not. It wasn't like I was saying I hadn't had any fun since I got married. In fact, Cosmas and I had plenty of fun—trying out restaurants with friends, window-shopping on Charles Street, and taking our dog to the Fresh Pond Reservoir on weekends.... Ah, defensive was now denial. Okay, so there were obviously different types of fun, but hey, nowhere in my vows did it state I was only allowed to partake in specific types of fun.

It was then that Cosmas called to tell me that he had safely arrived in Germany. Pleased with the distraction, I asked about his flight, what movies they showed, and whether or not his hotel TV carried any American channels (only CNN, but that didn't count). He asked whether I had any big plans for the weekend and I casually mentioned that Jenner might be in town. He took the news in stride, well knowing that Jenner and I were a force to be reckoned with back in the day, and told me that I deserved a girls' night out. Suddenly defensive again, I asked him if he was accusing me of shady dealings. Now he was defensive and asked whether he should be and what exactly the term "shady dealings" implied.

Responding to his question with a question of my own, I inquired whether he had ever felt like playing "single" (in quotations) for a night or two when he had been left on his own. It might have been the connection, but his pause seemed to go on a second longer than I would have liked. In a quiet voice he said that he almost never thought of his single life and was actually relieved to have it behind him. Before I could let out my sigh of relief, he continued to say that he had no problem with me playing "single" just as long as I knew that I was happily married while doing it. I told him that seemed reasonable to me, and he said he was glad and that he was now going to bed.

I called Jenner back at the end of the day and said I would freely admit that I was guilty of wanting to live vicariously through her for a night on the town, but that I never had any intention of leaving my ring at home. Then I told her that she would soon see that us married gals still knew how to have a good time. She said she was too busy to talk but she'd see me on Saturday.

I will spare you the total blow-by-blow of our girls' night out (and yes, I mean blow-by-blow figuratively, not literally), as I'm positive that most girls' nights are all pretty much the same, but the highlights include the following: wine, cigarettes, and getting ready to early Madonna; pink cocktails at Noir in the Charles Hotel; lots of toasts to ourselves (one naughty toast of "Cosmas who?"); more drinks at Jenner's fabulous gay client/friend's amazing loft in Kendall Square (with lots of oohing and aahing over his gorgeous pony-skin chaise lounge); dinner at the chi-chi 33, two bottles of wine, more cigarettes, a lengthy discussion of whether the one really hot guy at the bar was gay (vote was 2 to 2); the longest cab ride of my life back to Cambridge, which included lots of swaying (even though the radio wasn't on), repetitive references to "water," "coffee," "Advil," and inappropriate amounts of laughter over some silly princess pun I made up about Kir Royales; two more hours of squeals as we played exactly one song off of every CD I own; a chagrined drop-off of Carrie to her apartment across the hall (her boyfriend did not find her hard-core case of the giggles quite as amusing as we did), and finally giving in to sleep at close to 4:00 A.M. after a drowsy rehash of our good ol' college days.

The next morning, after surveying my no longer tidy apartment (the morning after a girls' night out, no matter if you're thirty-something or twenty-something, looks pretty much the same—clothes, makeup, and empty Diet Coke cans littered about—the two differences to note are that the cosmetics are now pricier and the new appearance of the all-important eye cream), I found myself thinking of Cosmas. As much as I was incredibly relieved that he wasn't due home until the next day (because expensive eye cream will only get you so far), I was also at the same time incredibly relieved that he *was* due home the next day. "Single" in quotations was certainly fun, but married (not in quotations) wasn't so bad either (and like I said, expensive eye cream will only get you so far).

SAYING BUH-BYE TO COOL

I'm not sure if I was ever cool, and surely the fact that I am thinking about it now means that if I was, I'm probably not anymore. Okay, I've now decided that I was once pretty cool, not cool like Bono is cool, but cool in the way a regular nonceleb can be. I was cool because I was confident. I was cool because I had once lived in New York. I was cool because I dressed well and accessorized even better. I was cool because I could make clever conversation and had the ability to mock myself in a way that others found amusing. Oh, and one more cool thing to note about me is that I smoke.

Okay, now before I have the entire antismoking lobby

breathing down my back, let me qualify this by saying that I think smoking is cool, and honestly, who the hell am I to know for sure (c'mon, we've already established that it's a toss-up whether or not I'm cool. So you people who think smoking is vile, you can say I'm uncool, and those of you who don't, well, if you're old enough to smoke then you're old enough to decide for yourselves).

Now, the one thing I want to make clear to all the people who think that smoking is a truly despicable habit is—all together now—we know. That's right, smokers may be fool-hardy when it comes to their future life spans, but we're not stupid. We have read the warning label that is printed on every pack. We have read all the articles in the media that list all the ways smoking is bad for you (your lungs, your heart, your skin, etc.). We have even heard the very sad stories of people dying from it, too. We know that a lot of people think smoking is disgusting. We know that tons of people don't even understand how anyone in their right mind could smoke. We know that parents are worried that their children will smoke (they should worry, because kids definitely think smoking is cool). We know—all together again—that smoking is bad.

But still, we smoke.

I picked up the habit fairly late, according to statistics. Most smokers start in high school, but I started in college. (Though I did once try to smoke in fifth grade with my friend Jodi out in the woods behind her house, but I'm pretty sure we weren't all that successful.) And, what's worse, I started smoking over a boy. Can you believe it? I guess there is no good reason to ever start smoking, so starting to smoke over a guy is probably on par with everything else. It was the summer after my freshman year of college and I was living on Avenue B with my friend Sarah in an incredibly small railroad apartment. There was a heat wave and we couldn't afford air-conditioning, so we spent a lot of time sitting in bars drinking Diet Coke (fake IDs never pass in New York) and talking about boys. In fact, to pass the time we constantly were daring each other to go up and talk to cute boys we didn't know (and who probably wouldn't date a college girl) just so the others could watch from the safety of our table. It was all harmless; well, at least it started out that way, but eventually it was my turn and the boy my friends picked out for me was a little cuter than I had hoped for. (The cuter the guy, the more it hurt when you got shot down.)

So this particular cute boy happened to be standing by himself at the bar smoking a cigarette. So when coming up with a game plan it seemed natural to everyone else that I should go and bum a cigarette from him. I distinctly remember telling them that this was a dumb idea because I didn't smoke, and I remember Sarah, who was a smoker herself, telling me that smoking was easy.

Smoking, when face-to-face with a cute stranger with three of your girlfriends watching your every move, is anything but easy. In fact, I made a total ass of myself. I did that classic sitcom move where I was completely awkward and klutzy without being cute. I dropped the one he gave me on the floor and was about to pick it up when I heard a faint squeal in the distance. (*Ohmygod, don't pick it up. Ew.*) I gratefully accepted a second one, and when he leaned in to light it for me we almost bonked heads. I'm pretty sure he was finding the whole thing amusing (after all, what cute guy doesn't like attention?), but he was less amused when I took a drag, choked, and proceeded to cough the smoke directly into his face. He turned away in surprise and horror (it goes without saying that I might have gotten some spit on him, yeah, I know, double ew), and I did what any humiliated girl would do in my place. I bolted.

That night when we couldn't sleep due to the heat, I made Sarah teach me to smoke. She was reluctant at first, but gave in when I reminded her that she was the one ("It's so easy") who was most responsible for the sudden ending of a perfectly good night out.

I watched her poke a small hole at the base of the cigarette, right above the filter. She explained that this would help make it less harsh, and would hopefully prevent a repeat of my earlier experience. (She had already washed her face for the night, so she was trying to avoid spit at all costs.) It took a while, but I finally got the hang of it. Sure it was nasty, but I was a woman on a mission. And when you're young, it's rare to ever think of the big-picture effect of your actions. (Few things are worse than getting your spit on a cute boy, at least one who didn't want it.)

In the beginning, and I'm sure it's the same with most smokers, I didn't classify myself as a real smoker, only a "social smoker." Which meant that I smoked only when I was out at bars. Unfortunately for me, I spent a lot of time out in bars, and pretty quickly went from a "social smoker" to someone who smoked every day. What's worse is that I liked it. I know it's hard for people who smoke to explain what they like about it, as I'm sure everyone has their own reasoning. Well, I'm not shy; one of the reasons I liked to smoke was because I thought it was cool. There, I said it. I'm sorry, but it looks cool, it makes you feel cool, and it makes others look cool.

Of course, there's also the appealing factor of it being terribly bad for you. It was a little illicit, but obviously not illicit enough to make you not want to do it.

I have certainly thought about quitting over the fourteen years that I have smoked, because it is expensive; because it is bad for me; because you can no longer smoke in bars and restaurants in New York, California, and Massachusetts; because I told my husband that I would; because I told my mom I would; and because I don't even enjoy it as much as I used to. I quit for a month once using Zyban, but it was never my intention to quit for good. I had only decided that my pack-a-day habit and my obvious physical addiction was probably something that I needed to regain control over. There are a lot of control issues involved in smoking, first being in control over your own body by choosing to do something bad for it, but eventually the tables turn and you realize that you're the one being controlled.

I'm aware that like most smokers, I have a tendency to make excuses about it. I can't quit; I'll gain weight. I can't quit; it's the only time I can take a break. And of course the main reason that I can't quit: because I just don't want to.

Time moves on, and now I'm in my thirties and I know I'm getting ready to give up the habit for good. For the last few years I cut back considerably, maybe smoking a pack every seven days or so. Some days I don't even smoke at all. I sometimes think that I will just naturally give it up, but I've been thinking that for a while and it hasn't happened yet. Giving up smoking, like smoking itself, is a very active thing. It's something that requires determination, the very same determination I had on that first night I learned to smoke. It's something that requires motivation, not from others but from myself.

In my head I tell myself that I will certainly quit when I make the choice to have children, which might be a bit of a cop-out, as I know I should make the choice for myself as opposed to another. But smoking isn't something that's logical (obviously, because it really is bad for you); no, it's more vague than that. I know I'm old enough to know better. But then again, I'm probably old enough to dismiss the notion of being cool, too.

Okay, how's this: Smoking is definitely not cool. It may look cool. It may seem cool. But it's just a big bad health-risk wolf in cool sheep's clothing. And me? Well, I guess when I smoke I'm not really cool either, and in fact, maybe I never was. (Wow, it's pretty cool to admit to being uncool. I knew it. I'm cool—still not cool like Bono, but cool enough to know I'll stop smoking when I'm good and ready.)

CELLULOID FEVER

Right now, as I write this, I am totally and completely up-to-date on all the gossip in the United States. I know it's a bold statement to make, that I'm totally current, but that's the way I feel. I feel full, maxed out, and fairly appalled that it is even possible to feel this way. I mean, the new *Us Weekly*, *People*, *In Touch*, and *Star* are probably at the presses right now, or in fact are bundled on trucks and are being delivered now, but I know for a fact they're not at any of my local newsstands yet, nor are they in my mailbox (I'm a subscriber to *Us*), *or* at my local library.

I'm a fan of the Internet, of course, and can barely remember what it was like not to have E-mail, Google, or IMDb, but right now I'm pretty sure I'm up-to-date on that, too. You see, I am a media junkie, perhaps not too surprising, since I was raised in a mass-media world. I *adore* magazines—hell, I devour them. And I am a huge movie fan; I *live* for Fridays, when the new releases come out. I love TV, too, and could not be held responsible for my actions if something happened to my TiVo. It goes without saying that I'm a book lover, too, though it's surprising that I still have the time or the attention span to read anything that doesn't have a picture to accompany it.

I'm not proud of this, but neither do I think it's necessarily a bad thing. Sure, if I really think about it, it's obvious that my time could be better spent *doing* things, as opposed to reading about other people doing things. In fact, it's almost fascinating that I can manage to care about these people I read about, because I certainly don't have a real relationship with them (and I'm just not that into "imaginary relationships" at this point). I know that stars are harassed by the press all the time, and I'm sure it must be annoying not to have any real private life, but at the same time I don't really feel too bad for any of them. I mean, c'mon, they're well paid for their troubles. (In fact, I have a small bone to pick with Madonna, whom I've always admired, because this newfound allegiance to the U.K. simply flies in the face of the fact that it was the American people who loved her first! I mean, it was people like you and me who gave her bank the boost she needed to really *become* a material girl and not just squirm around *singing* about it. Right? Don't worry, Madge, I'm not *that* mad.)

I wonder whether I'd be happier and have higher self-esteem if I turned my back on media altogether. It must be something like porn, which I don't really get, by the way—I mean, what's the point of looking at these gorgeous pictures of women doing God only knows what and wearing next to nothing? Surely most guys know that they will never ever have a shot at having sex with these women. Ever. But I've heard the stories and I guess I get the whole fantasy aspect of it. Or take alcohol—I'm personally not a big drinker, but sometimes, after a particularly crappy day, I can relate to this need to get a little numb and escape your everyday life.

So okay, I suppose my love of media is basically just an escape from my everyday existence. Though I do wonder whether perhaps this is spelling out a larger problem with my life—you know, the fact that I feel the need to escape so often. Truth be told, my everyday life is actually pretty good. I'm lucky enough to get paid to do a job that I love. I have a fabulous dog that loves me and keeps me company. I have a wonderful family that I'm thankful for (albeit a dysfunctional one, but then show me a family that isn't). A cute husband that can pull off a beard and a potbelly (so unfair). And last, but not least, I have some really great friends. (No, no—I mean in addition to Rachel, Ross, and Monica, whom I still cherish even in reruns.)

What is it about *Vogue* magazine that I find so satisfying? I have long since given up the childish dreams of wanting to be a model (I'm five feet four inches tall). I really don't have the bank account to afford most of the clothes that they showcase. I enjoy reading the articles, but I also know perfectly well that they aren't going to change my life (and I'm also aware of the fact that most of them aren't completely true; never believe a star who says she can eat anything she wants without gaining weight, because it's a lie).

Before I wrote books I worked in marketing and public relations so I'm pretty hip to the whole notion that the United States has a problem with consumer goods. I mean there is just too much, even for me, and I'm a girl who loves to shop. Sometimes I feel like a hamster on a wheel, going round and round each day, week, month with the newest magazines. There is and there always will be a new "it" girl, movie, book, blouse.... It's endless, and you can never begin to hope to keep up with it all.

There have been pockets of time when something was going on in my life that kept me away from the media for a few weeks at a time; at first I always get a little panicky that I'm missing out (withdrawal can be ugly). After a while, though, I don't really miss it. But I always go back, and right when I get back into the thick of it, I always have the moment where I'm like, "How bizarre, it's like I never *left*."

There will always be that star who just broke up with her boyfriend; there will always be that actor who knocked up his model girlfriend; there will always be that pair of shoes you know would really look great (well, with the right outfit, of course, and handbag). There will always be blockbuster movies; there will always be a new TV show that fails—whether it's unexpected or the train wreck that anyone could have seen coming; and there will always be that overlooked book that just doesn't quite get the readership it deserves....

This continuity can make you feel a whole number of different ways: cynical, secure, jaded, hopeful, and even resolute. Our own lives, too, if we observe them from a distance, follow a similarly circular path. Sure, we move forward in age, get a little farther up the ladder at work, but a lot of things stay the same. I will *always* be a procrastinator, even though it makes me crazy. I will *always* be a reluctant gym member. I will *always* be on some form of diet, even when I swear that I'm going to give up my dream of being a Skinny Bitch. And of course the drama of our everyday lives will always be there too—friends getting divorced, your brother becoming a father, you accidentally backing up into a parked car (oops).

I know a lot of people are obsessed with celebrities because they wish to be just like them; but that's not the case for me (well, I would like their thighs). I'm not really *interested* in living someone else's life, because mine is just fine. My life is not exactly fabulous, I guess. And I am certainly not crazy rich. But there is plenty that could be a whole helluva lot worse. For example, my thighs *could* be even bigger than they are now, and my ass *could* be even wider than a Mack truck. Or, worse yet, I could have this skinny bitch of a stomach that requires at least five hundred sit-ups a day.

THE TAMAGOTCHI GOTCHA

I'd be lying if I didn't say that the thought of having a baby terrifies me a little. I mean, sometimes I'm still shocked that I'm a wife; so obviously, adding "mother" to my title is a bit daunting. I suppose my feelings might stem from the days that I feel less than competent as an adult in general, so being responsible for a baby who is completely dependent on me makes me a tiny bit nervous.

Sometimes I share my anxiety with my friend Stephanie, who had a baby at the age of thirty, and is the only woman I know who still seems to be pretty much the same person after the fact. (As opposed to some harried stressed-out baby-talking Super Mom who always seems on the brink of breakdown; I won't mention names, even though there's no way they'd have the time to read this book anyway.) Stephanie empathizes with my worries and explains that there is hardly a day that goes by when she, herself, doesn't wonder if she's a fit mom. She says that once you're in the situation, it's like anything else, and you just deal with it as best you can.

I'm pretty sure it was during one of these phone calls that we got on the topic of that hokey high school home-economics experiment that you sometimes see portrayed on sitcoms, although you have never met anyone who has actually done it. Y'know, the one where the students had to "mother" an egg for a few days, thereby teaching them the value of parenting, or maybe it was just a cloaked lesson in safe sex. Anyway, we had a good laugh at the picture of me carrying around an egg for a few days to see how I'd fare as a mom. But later, after we ended our call (with Stephanie sweetly letting me know that I could borrow her daughter whenever I wanted, too), I thought about it some more and decided that maybe it wasn't such a silly idea after all.

Since we now live in the age of technology, I knew that using a real egg would no longer be necessary. After a few minutes on Amazon.com, I located an electronic Tamagotchi toy, which is basically an electronic baby. Tamagotchis were a big deal when I was a preteen, but they had lately made a comeback with the five-to-ten set and had also been vastly improved. The Tamagotchis of today now had infrared capability so that once you raised your egg into a little electronic "person" you could actually mate it with another Tamagotchi and raise a second generation. I purchased two and paid the extra fifteen bucks for overnight delivery.

The next night I was stretched out in bed trying to make sense of the page of directions, which might as well have been written in Japanese, when Cosmas came home from work. Seeing me in pajamas with some new toy was not something that gave Cosmas a moment's pause, as he was used to my compulsive shopping behavior (though he'd be pissed if he knew I paid for express delivery; oh well). It was only later, when he was ready for bed, that he inquired what was so fascinating about what he assumed was just a new key chain (which wasn't exactly inaccurate, since the Tamagotchi actually did double as a key ring).

While I explained my little sociological experiment to him, I watched as he struggled to keep his eyes focused on me, as opposed to letting them roll up into his head. It was clear that he wasn't in the mood to discuss why I was embarking on this electronic adventure in the first place (though you'd have to be a moron not to know; I mean, I was twenty-five years older than the recommended age for the toy). But this was fine, because I was obviously conflicted on the topic myself. Though I did share with him the intricacies involved, which were that at the touch of a few buttons a little egg would appear (black meant boy, white meant girl), and then after a few minutes a little blob would show up which was the baby phase. And during the baby phase you had to feed the baby bottles, clean up its "poo," and of course play with the baby, too. After about a day, the baby would turn into a toddler, which involved pretty much the same thing as the baby, except that he was now eating food nuggets and there were also snacks. You were also given the ability to give your boy or girl praise and discipline, depending on the situation. According to the instructions, it could also get sick, which would require you to administer medicine via a different button. Eventually, the toddler would grow into a teenager, and so on and so forth. When I got to the part about mating them and growing a whole electronic family, Cosmas stopped me, gently advising that I was maybe getting a little ahead of myself.

Point taken. Even though I was eager to begin, I did realize it was late and it might be better to start off fresh in the morning. Lying in bed in the dark, I thought about what I was doing, and even though I knew the whole thing was pretty random on my part, I couldn't help but feel nervous. I mean, it was possible that I would fail miserably (yes, it's possible to have your Tamagotchi die). Eventually, I convinced myself that since the toy was geared toward kids much younger than myself, I'd probably have a six times better chance at handling it. I mean, after all, I had raised a pretty swell dog—one that was a little spoiled and headstrong, but at least he knew I was his mom.

The next morning I hatched my egg at my local Starbucks. It was a boy, and I named him Zeus. After a few moments of watching my little egg pulsate on the tiny screen, he hatched into a baby, resembling a small happy face. I fed him a bottle immediately and then checked his happiness meter, which consisted of four little empty hearts. Hmmm. Obviously, food was not enough to make him happy. I hit the praise button and checked again. Nothing. I played with him, which consisted of hitting another button that made him jump up and down. I checked the happy meter and now had one filled-in heart. I was ecstatic.

I put him in my pocket and headed out. On the way home Zeus beeped, and in the middle of Mass Ave, I pulled him out and noticed a small pile of excrement on the screen. With the touch of a button I cleaned it up, and was soon confronted with honking horns. Looking up, I found myself still standing in the middle of the street and realized that if I didn't move quickly, me and Zeus might end up as roadkill.

The rest of the morning went pretty smoothly. I stared at the screen, fed him, played with him, praised him, and cleaned up his poop. I was amazed at how quickly the day went when you were obsessively checking in on a baby, albeit a digital one.

By the evening I had two filled-in hearts and was getting a little cocky about my mothering skills. I called Stephanie to tell her about Zeus, and she told me that the feeding and cleaning up poo cycle pretty much summed up life with a newborn. It was at that moment when I heard a faint beep. *Oh no, has Zeus been beeping for a while now and I have been too self-absorbed on the phone to even notice? Crap. I suck at this. Ah, how quickly the mighty fall.* This was the point where I began to sound frazzled and distracted in the same way some of my other friends who were mothers sometimes get with me, where they pretend they are listening, but what they're really doing is giving ninety-eight percent of their brain waves to dealing with their baby. Finally, I realized I needed the other two percent as well, because I was having a problem locating where I put little Zeus. (Yes,

I know how bad that sounds, but the thing is like two inches, for Pete's sake.)

Stephanie understood totally (though I'm sure she got a good laugh at my expense, but hey, what are friends for?).... So now I was on my hands and knees, wondering whether Zeus had fallen on the floor or into the couch crack. Wendell, my dog, was soon by my side because he assumed that I was on the floor to play with him.

"Wendell, not now. Mommy is busy," I told him.

Wendell, of course had no idea what I was saying, because in his two short years of life, it was pretty rare that Mommy was ever too busy to play with him. In fact, Mommy probably could have written an entire novel in the time she had spent playing with him.

"WENDELL. NOT NOW!"

Wendell understood that, and his ears fell, and his little tail drooped, and he looked really upset. It's rare that I scold him. Okay, that's a lie, I am actually sort of a strict doggy mommy (though really generous with new toys and long walks), but I never scold for no apparent reason, like today. Like now.

Zeus beeped. Again.

Dammit! Where was the little bastard?

I am the Tazmanian Devil now, a whirling dervish slamming through the apartment trying to find my electronic baby, which is probably starving, covered in poo, and has four empty hearts on his happy meter.

I found him ten minutes later with the mail (if only Zeus could read, I'm sure he'd have been happy tucked away in my new issue of *Entertainment Weekly*). I was right, though. Zeus was not amused by the disappearance of his mother. I cleaned the poo. I fed him two bottles (which I'm sure you're not supposed to do, but oh well), and I played with him over and over and over. I also praised the hell out of him. I was given no love on the happy meter. None. Great, I had raised an unforgiving and cold little smiley face. Perfect.

That night, Cosmas decided to just ignore me and my bad mood, because there is probably nothing on record in the history of mankind that would tell him what to do when his wife is upset over the state of her relationship with her electronic toy baby. Zeus was FINALLY asleep and I now had him attached to my jeans so I wouldn't lose the little bugger again. I had tried my best to make it up to Wendell, but of course he saw right through me. I'm sure he had no idea what I found so interesting about a little piece of plastic, and let's just say he wasn't amused over not having my undivided attention. Meanwhile, it was close to midnight and I was exhausted. I then tried to figure out what I had managed to accomplish that day besides caring for Zeus; I came up with a big fat zero. I did not get to the dry cleaners. I did not get to the grocery store. I did not manage to get into the freakin' shower, even. Little Zeus, or at least my intense neuroses over little Zeus, were kickin' my sorry ass.

I'm not big into dreams—meaning I don't tend to remember them that often, nor do I put much stock in them in general. Of course, I hate when people tell me their dreams (unless they are weird sex dreams—those I like to hear about), so I hate to bore you with my dreams. But I feel I must. So in my dream I was trapped inside a Ms. Pac-Man maze, and of course I had lost Pac-Man (i.e., Zeus) and I was running all over the maze trying to find him, while those stupid little ghost munchkin things were chasing me. It was most unpleasant. I woke up once in the middle of the night convinced I heard a beep, but when I finally found Zeus, still attached to my jeans, which were crumpled on the floor, I saw that the screen was dark and there were little Zs appearing to show that he was fast asleep. Thank God, at least one of us was getting a good night's rest.

I'm pleased to report that the next morning went very well, and my darling baby Zeus grew up into a toddler. I felt like I had just graduated; it was great. Now he was a bigger blob, and there was a new game that I could play with him, which consisted of him jumping over little hurdles. I, not being all that coordinated, wasn't very good at timing, so I only managed to guide him over the first hurdle, but c'mon, we can't all raise Olympic athletes, and it's not like I was all that coordinated in athletics myself. Maybe Zeus would grow up to be a Nobel prize–winning author. Yes, that's right, I could start living out my dreams through him. Hell, maybe Zeus would become a photographer who worked for a tabloid paper and I could get all the gossip early.

After two lattes (normally I only need one) I managed to get through my morning in a fairly orderly fashion. I fed him. I cleaned up after him. I praised him. I disciplined him (don't want him to get too spoiled), and by the evening his happiness meter read two and a half hearts. Rock on, Mom!

I had even made a special trip to Petco and bought Wendell a bunch of new toys, so he had basically forgiven me as well. (Yes, I had learned something from my mom. Got a sulky kid? Throw a little green at the problem, and all will be better soon.)

Cosmas even took a bit more interest in Zeus that night and I showed him how Zeus was now two years old and thriving. Cosmas gave me a pat on the back for my accomplishments; I beamed. He also told me that he had never once doubted my mothering skills, which made me cry (I'm not normally the crying type, but I had had two more lattes in the afternoon to keep myself awake and now I was a bit overwrought from all the caffeine).

On Day 3, Zeus woke up in a bad mood. Or at least I assumed it was a bad mood, because he had a dark little cloud over him. It looked like he was breathing hard (surely he hadn't learned how to smoke, right?), and the happiness meter was on empty. I wondered if he had slept badly. I wondered if he had had a bad dream. I wondered if he was sick. There is a little "medicine" button, and I pushed it once. It didn't work. I pushed it again. The dark cloud disappeared, but the heavy breathing remained. I tried not to worry about it too much, as I read in the instructions that there would be times when my Tamagotchi just wouldn't feel that well. I knew there was nothing more that I could do except be careful to monitor him every half hour or so. I rationalized that there was no way that some little snot-nosed seven-year-old kid could have the attention span to give their Tamagotchi any more tender loving care than I was currently giving Zeus. I mean, I didn't have to go to second grade. I didn't have to take naps. Boy, Zeus sure was lucky to have a thirty-three-year-old for a mom instead of a little girl who still wore a Hello Kitty watch. (Okay, full disclosure, I had a Hello Kitty watch too, but I also had a real Tag Heuer grown-up-person watch, too.)

Forget what I said earlier about taking a nap, because that afternoon I became so incredibly tired that I zonked out on the couch for a good three hours. I slept like the dead. No dreams, and obviously no hearing skills, because by the time I woke up, Wendell was whining and Zeus was beeping. I had totally slept through Wendell's normal afternoon walk time (whoops) and I was scared to see Zeus's happiness meter; I wondered if I could get demerits. I rushed out the door with Wendell, and as I was running down the front steps I checked on Zeus. Uh-oh. There was a little skull-and-crossbones floating above his head. Holy cow! There was no way this could be good. At first I thought he was dead, but then I remembered that the info packet said that if I killed my Tamagotchi it would turn into an angel with wings.

I gave Zeus three doses of medicine. I pressed the "praise" button over and over. I fed him a meal and gave him two snacks...and let him dance around for fun. Mr. Skullface disappeared, but the black cloud and the heavy breathing were back.

JESUS! WHAT MORE DO YOU WANT? JUST TELL ME WHAT YOU WANT? I'LL DO ANYTHING.

I was now in the dog park near my house, and Wendell had been happily running around the field with a stick in his mouth, but when I screamed he promptly dropped his stick and gave me a quizzical look—the look that said, *Oh brother, Mommy's off her rocker.*

I called Stephanie and got her voice mail. DAMMIT! I thought about calling Cosmas, but then I'd have to admit that I let our electronic child fall sick while I was sacked out on the couch for the entire afternoon. UGH. I called my brother, John, in Philly. He was a doctor, and I have always said (because it's true) that he had a much better bedside manner than Cosmas anyway.

Of course, I was loath to explain the whole backstory to my big brother, so I just told him that I had a "friend" who had a sick toddler. He asked how sick. I said I didn't know, because the toddler couldn't talk so it was hard to know. He asked what hurt. The head? The stomach? What? I said I wasn't sure, but that I knew my "friend" had given him medicine, a lot of medicine, and he still wasn't better. This was when my brother got a bit suspicious, because when he asked what kind of medicine I choked and didn't know what to say, so I said, "I dunno, just medicine that makes you better." So then my brother asked what friend I was talking about (as he knew most of my friends), so I said it was Stephanie. My brother didn't buy this for one second because Stephanie's dad was a doctor, and he knew she wasn't a moron (even though she was friends with me).

After a couple more big fat lies on my part, I broke down. Yes, in the dog park sitting on a bench, I had to swallow what was left of my pride and confess to my brother that my electronic baby, Zeus, was sick and I didn't know what to do.

The pause was so long, you probably would have to call it something else. My brother, like my husband, was somewhat used to my wacky smart-but-oh-so-dumb ideas, so he didn't bother to question the whole experiment, and in fact, he was probably as nice as one could be given the situation (i.e., he didn't mock me or laugh at me while on the phone). Instead, he put on his best doctor's voice and told me that sometimes, with a sick, ahem, child, you just had to let whatever "illness" it had just run its course.

"What if he dies?"

He sighed. "I doubt he's going to die."

"How do you know?"

Sigh number two. "I don't, but it'd be sort of a downer toy if the thing died when you've been taking such good care of it."

"But I fell asleep! I'm a bad mom."

He must have been out of sighs, because I didn't get a third. "You are not a bad mom. Look at Wendell."

OHMYGOD, WENDELL. WHERE'S MY DOG?

I dropped the phone and realized that for the last ten minutes I hadn't once even so much as looked up to see where my darling dog was. *I should be put away.*

I scanned the whole park for his little furry frame. Nothing. Oh my God, my life was over. I decided that I needed to start running, but I wasn't sure where I should run to, which was when I began to run in place. This was when I stepped on Wendell's foot. (Wendell had been lying under the bench eating a stick.) Wendell squealed. I screamed. Zeus went flying into the grass. Wendell ran and grabbed

Zeus in his mouth and bolted down the field (at least I didn't break his foot).

That was it. Game over. I had completely lost control of my entire life. I crumpled to the ground in defeat, and reached for my phone. My brother, surprisingly, was still on the phone.

He sighed again. "Do I even want to know?"

I told him no, that he wouldn't even believe it if I told him.

He then said, "For what it's worth, motherhood is supposed to be hard and scary, and the thing to remember is that even if you are clueless, so is everyone else."

I thanked him for his weird backward compliment and told him I'd call him later.

Wendell, not quite sure why I wasn't chasing him down to retrieve what he had taken, was now back by my side.

In my best stern voice I told him to drop it. And, surprisingly, he did.

I rubbed the dog spit off on my jeans and was pleased to see that he hadn't actually chewed on the Tamagotchi, so it wasn't broken.

I peered at the little screen and the black cloud and the heavy breathing were gone. In fact, Zeus looked almost happy to be back with me. His happiness meter read one heart. Hell, I'll take it. By God, I've earned it.

NOTE: *Zeus died on Day 5. Cause of death was unknown. I could have hatched another egg and started again, but I just didn't have the heart. The late great Zeus is now being used as a key chain.*

THE SIREN SONG
OF SUBURBIA

It goes without saying that as a hard-core urbanite, I have a tendency to make fun of the suburbs. It just goes with the territory, and I graciously accept that there are plenty of people who could never understand the appeal of city living—in fact, when I was back in Tennessee for holidays when I was in college (I was attending New York University), one of my father's colleagues, who was born, raised, and certainly sure to die in small-town Tennessee, told me that he'd rather have his back broke in hell than live in New York. I laughed it off, and politely replied that New York wasn't for everyone.

Sometimes I wonder why I'm so intent on leading a big-city life. Sure there are days when it is a holy nightmare—

what with the lines, the traffic, and the fact that you can go days without seeing any green. But I thrive on the energy that cities provide, with the throngs of people always rushing to go places—and most importantly, there are places to go. To me the city is about having options—meaning that there are a thousand places to go on a Friday night—and I am happy just knowing that, even when I choose to stay at home. It is a peaceful feeling to be doing nothing by choice, just as long as you know that there is also plenty to do.

I was a total wild child in high school—but remember, this was the late '80s in a Podunk Southern town, so what was wild then (sneaking out and driving around dark country roads in the middle of the night) was not on par with what's "wild" for teenagers now (do we even want to know?). Anyway, I think my willful capriciousness came down to just wanting more. Small towns offer very little in the way of entertainment. We had one local movie theater that showed only two movies at a time. We had a small strip that the high school kids cruised, and most nights the big hangout was parking your car in the large Kroger's parking lot and just complaining with your friends that there was nothing else to do.

But as I get older, I'm starting to understand more and more why some people eventually leave the city. These days, it's a much rarer occasion that I'm out on the town past midnight, and yes, I've even been guilty of not wanting to go places strictly because I know there will be too many people, especially too many young people who will be almost vibrating with the desire for more, new, different. I still have pangs of those feelings every now and again, especially when there's nothing good on HBO, and sure I talk a big game about the great restaurants and bars I could frequent, if only I weren't so tired.

Maybe that's why people leave the city for the burbs; maybe sometimes the abundance of too much choice becomes a burden and you'd rather have fewer things to choose from when faced with your rapidly shrinking free time.

My first friend to leave city life was Stephanie. And it happened really fast. One day I got a phone call that she was pregnant and getting married in two months to her long-time live-in boyfriend. A few more months passed and she had a baby girl and they were moving to Annapolis, Maryland, where they had bought a house. I'm sure she was heartbroken to leave the city, because she, like me, had lived there since college, but she didn't tell me this. In fact, she seemed excited with the prospect of having a house of her own, a yard, and a new BMW station wagon. As the time passed by she told me that small-town living wasn't half bad; sure, she missed the city, but not as much as she thought she would. She told me that she was actually too busy with the baby to have much time to think about it, and that she had even less time to go out.

The first time I visited I couldn't get over how much space she had. I was now living in Cambridge, Massachusetts, and had traded up to a bigger apartment myself, but a house is an altogether different beast. She had a basement with a washer/dryer; she had a small backyard off the kitchen; she had a formal dining room, proper living room, and two more floors to boot. I checked her face for signs of longing, but I didn't find much. Instead we spent a lot of time on her front porch (oh yeah, she had one of those, too) and drank coffee and smoked cigarettes and rehashed our twenties.

I will say that I certainly felt very grown-up that day, hanging out with my friend who was now a mother, and laughing that we were ever so young. Her husband made steaks that night, and we ate like real grown-ups at their dining-room table. We had adult conversations, too—talking about the environment, the public-school systems, and the fact that keeping up a house was a lot of work. After a very relaxing weekend, where I did not once think about city life, I sat on the train and wondered whether I, too, could adapt to nonurban living as easily. At the time, I decided, no, I probably wouldn't, and came up with hundreds of reasons why the city was better. But I was a little less sure.

The next to leave the city was Laura. She had married a year after me, got pregnant in her second year, and moved a half hour out of New York to Maplewood, New Jersey. I wasn't totally shocked, because of course we had talked about it ahead of time, but I was still surprised at how fast it all happened. I tried not to play devil's advocate by saying something like "YOU'RE MOVING TO NEW JERSEY? WHY THE HELL WOULD YOU LEAVE NEW YORK FOR NEW JERSEY?" And instead, I did what any best friend would do: I gave her a big congratulations and told her I was sure that it would be great. After I hung up the phone, I of course wigged out a little. Not because I didn't agree with her decision—obviously, it was her life and her decision—but more because it made me question even more my own decisions.

I had moved out of New York right when I got married, but it was pretty much by force, because I didn't do it willingly. In my first two years of living in the Boston area, there was not a single day that went by that I didn't think about New York. Sure Boston is a major metropolitan city, but it's no New York. Two more years have passed and we are approaching the end of our stay (we had made a deal that after five years I would get to pick our next place to live), and where I was once so sure that we were definitely going straight back to New York, I am now less sure. I still miss it, but being away from it I have more perspective to see some of the negatives of living in Manhattan.

First off, I'm not rich, and when you're single and twenty-something and don't have much money, it doesn't really matter. But now that I'm older and much more realistic about how much things cost (and that you can't just charge everything on your credit cards), I can see where living in New York can take away some of your options as opposed to offering them. The housing market is legendary in New York, and when you're there it's easier to go along with the crazy prices. But when you don't live there it's pretty hard to swallow that a million-dollar mortgage (which you can't even afford) will only get you two bedrooms, and that's if you're lucky. So not only are you not going to be able to give your dog a yard (probably ever), you might not be able to give your future kids their own bedrooms, and don't even get me started on the costs of education.

I believe the number one reason that people leave big cities is because they want a better quality of life. I never really understood what that meant, because intellectually it seems that any city can provide a richer life experience (more culture, more restaurants, more different types of people), but now I'm starting to see the light a little more. (Let's be honest, what five-year-old would rather go to MoMA as opposed to playing on a swing set in their own backyard?)

When I visited Laura's new house I knew that she had made the right decision for herself. She had a lovely home with a lot of space and a beautiful baby boy who certainly deserved the big yard that he would one day get to run around in. Yes, we spent some time on her large back porch talking about everything we missed about New York City, but we spent even more time talking about our own futures, which seemed equally as big and full of possibilities.

I'm not sure whether I'm ever going to give up city living myself. I'm not at a stage in my life when I can say that suburban living is a better or worse choice. Sure I would kill for my own washer and dryer, and God knows, maybe my apartment wouldn't be so cluttered if, oh, I had a little more room, but I still enjoy sitting on my couch in a big city knowing that there is something pretty damn big waiting for me, if I'm so inclined to go and see.

CHECKING IT TWICE

At the ripe old age of twenty-four, my friend Stephanie and I sat in her West Village apartment and decided it was high time we stopped having endless discussions about our future lives and actually figured some things out. We armed ourselves with a pot of coffee, a pack of smokes, and a bright yellow self-help book that was titled along the lines of *You Can Do Anything If Only You Knew What the Hell You Wanted to Do*. We liked the book because it had little exercises in it, and since we were only a couple of years out of college we still believed that a lot could be solved with a sharp number-two pencil and a pad of paper.

Stephanie was in charge of sitting on the couch and flipping through the chapters and reading passages aloud, while my job was to nod a lot and say things like "That sounds reasonable" and "Wow, maybe there's something to this self-help crap after all?" (I was also in charge of finding the appropriate Madonna songs to keep us motivated.) After a half hour of this, we finally settled on an exercise where you were supposed to divide up your life into five-year increments and say what you would like to have accomplished by that age going all the way up to the age of ninety-five.

The easiest part, of course, was recording what we had accomplished up to this point in our lives, which amounted to learning to tie one's shoe, riding bicycles, learning the value of friends, surviving our teenage years, getting into college, finishing college, and finally getting our first jobs in book publishing (we met at a *Paris Review* party, delighted over the fact that we were wearing the same black Chaiken skinny pants, and soon became smoking book-party partners in crime).

One of the pitfalls of spending your twenties in a city like New York was that it made you believe that you could really do anything, and I believe that we actually thought that we could choreograph our future lives on a legal pad, and that all it took was a little effort. (But then again, we also believed that we would both one day be able to whip out a great American novel with ease as soon as we managed to get rid of our day jobs.)

In our efforts to impress each other, we really got ambitious with our future accomplishments, and among the things that made the list—beyond the basics of marrying

Mr. Right, buying a fabulous apartment on lower Fifth Avenue, and (maybe) having kids—were things like going back to grad school (me for psychology, Steph for anthropology); writing not only one great literary novel but also having the wherewithal to not be labeled a one-hit wonder and churning out books every few years; writing a Broadway play (me); being a professor (Steph); choosing a second home (I picked the country, Stephanie picked the beach); endless traveling (I wanted to tackle the U.S. first, while Stephanie wanted to tackle the whole globe); finding a truly fulfilling hobby (I wanted to become a sculptress, Stephanie wanted to learn to play an instrument)...And then, suddenly, we were both in our fifties and then we looked around at our lives as they actually stood. We realized that we still had a long way to go, which we found a bit unsettling.

So then we pulled out all the stops and really got creative. We decided that everything we had done so far was pretty much all about ourselves, so we decided that it was now time to turn our attention to others, too. Well, we decided that acquiring a third house abroad might be sort of amusing, as well, and of course learning a second language would surely kill five years (I picked Greece, Stephanie picked Costa Rica). I decided that I would start a foundation that would introduce troubled teens to the creative arts (half the battle of being an artist was to be angst-ridden anyway), and Stephanie talked about following in Jane Goodall's footsteps and working with animals. We decided that we would probably have grandchildren by our sixties, so we gave a few years over to annoying our grown children by spoiling their hyperdisciplined kids. In our seventies we decided that it might be fun to live with other old people, so we decided to check ourselves in to some fabulous retirement place in Arizona or New Mexico. I would be the activities director and bully everyone into putting on productions of Tennessee Williams plays, and Stephanie could run the book club. In our eighties we decided it was time to get rid of all the money we had earned, because we decided that our ungrateful kids (who never once made it to our annual holiday spectacular where we would make the audience dress up as pumpkins, leaves, and turkeys) didn't deserve to get rich off our own work, and should find a way to make their own money. So we set up scholarship funds, gave to the ASPCA, and gave the balance to anyone hungry in foreign countries (by hungry we obviously didn't mean those dieting).

My most vivid memory of that day was looking down at our now lengthy list and cavalierly telling Stephanie that I was ready to call it quits in my nineties, because, honestly, by then if we had accomplished everything we had put down on paper, we would probably be a little tired. She agreed with me, and we decided that it was fine to kick off at ninety, right after we got a lot of plastic surgery so we would look good in our caskets.

We were a little dazed after we finished, but we were also proud, because we now had an outline of our future lives. I checked the book to find out what we were supposed to have gained from the exercise and realized that we hadn't exactly done it correctly (oops), though we had ended up at the same conclusion—which is life is much longer than you think it is. And that however old and terribly sophisticated we might have thought we were, we were not quite as washed up as we might have thought. And given that we were clearly going to be very busy for the next seventy or so years, we probably better squeeze in a little fun while we could. And so soon we were sipping margaritas at the Grange Hall.

Now, ten years have gone by and the Grange Hall is gone too, and interestingly enough I am more or less on track, I suppose, in that I am married and have already published a few books (albeit not the award-winning great American novel that was made into a movie with Brad Pitt, but sometimes it's okay to round up). Granted, I don't have the fabulous lower Fifth Avenue apartment yet, but now that I know a thing or two about mortagages, I would certainly revise the list and push that goal a bit further back. Say twenty years or so.

This is the point where I'm supposed to lay some hard-earned wisdom down on the table and say how much I've learned in the last ten years. You know, that I really knew nothing in my twenties. I suppose I could go on and on about how foolish I was to have such big ambitions when I knew so little about the cost of living, why it's important to have savings, and that I should know what the interest rates are on my credit cards, but I'm not going to, because it's not really true. And, in fact, yes, I guess I'm more mature now; I *have* learned a great deal through trial and error (lots of error). But I'm not quite ready to give up any of my grand plans for the future. I mean, who says that I can't still be ambitious in my goals? Who says I don't have what it takes to start a freakin' revolution?

In your twenties it's very easy to get caught up in all the excitement of anything being possible (especially while living in a place that's known for just that), and in your thirties it's very easy to settle in to a quieter sort of life in which you start to just accept things for what they are, rather than struggling for the new. Now, granted, I've had my moments of acceptance in the past few years, telling myself that I should just learn to be happy with everything that I have and that I shouldn't feel bad that I now truly believe that TiVo has changed my life. But now I know that my inner rebel was just resting, gathering up my strength (I didn't get much sleep in my twenties), and there are days when I wake up and I feel it's time to get back in the action again. Sure, I don't have the stamina that I once had, but I'm hardly ready for shuffleboard on the lido deck, either.

I decided it was time to redraft my life plan to the age of ninety-five again, and I spent a few hours at my kitchen table with a pad of paper and a pencil. There were definitely some changes to my list—a little less real-estate ownership (at least I don't *think* you can buy a second home with a credit card), and a little more giving to others (I guess I'm not as selfish as I thought I was)—but otherwise I kept all of my big-ticket goals. I still want to write that novel. I still want to write that play (though off-Broadway would be fine). I'd love to write and sell a screenplay, and I have a new goal to get involved in television, too, as I now know there isn't much good TV on Friday and Saturday nights.

As to whether or not I'll accomplish everything on my list, I don't know. But I *do* know that I have plenty of time. And I also know that ninety-five doesn't sound half bad anymore.

Now, if I can just make it through the second half of my thirties...

Acknowledgments

For once in my life I'm going to try to go short and sweet. There are so many people that need to be thanked when it comes to this book; hell, there are so many people I need to say thank you to when it comes to who I am today.

I hope you all know how important you are to me, how much I cherish my family, friends, everyone who supports my writing, and, of course, all the random people (especially women) who inspire me every single day. Yes, I'm a woman who has a very big appetite for life and all it has to offer, but I also know what truly makes one's life full (no, I'm not talking about pancakes)—it's simple really. Hell, even though I don't cook, I'll throw out a recipe. Lots of love. Lots of laughs. Mix in those you want to share love and laughter with. Repeat daily. (Add sprinkles, whipped cream, cherries . . . don't forget, happy calories don't count.)

About the Author

JENNY LEE was born in Tennessee, spent her twenties in Manhattan, moved to Cambridge, Massachusetts, and recently moved back to New York City. She writes for *Animal Fair*, *Redbook*, and the *Boston Globe Sunday Magazine*. She is also the author of *I Do. I Did. Now What?!* and *What Wendell Wants*.